WE WILL NOT DANCE ON OUR GRANDPARENTS' TOMBS

INDIGENOUS UPRISINGS IN ECUADOR

Kintto Lucas

Translated by Dinah Livingstone

First published 2000
Catholic Institute for International Relations (CIIR)
Unit 3 Canonbury Yard
190a New North Road
London N1 7BJ, UK

A CIP catalogue record for this book is available from the British Library
ISBN 1852872365 (pbk)

Translated from the Spanish (*La Rebelión de los Indios*)
by Dinah Livingstone
La Rebelión de los Indios, published by Abya Yala, Quito (2000)

English translation edited by: Adam Bradbury, CIIR
Design: Boldface, London
Printing: Russell Press Ltd, Nottingham
Cover picture: Associated Press
Funding for the translation into English was provided by CAFOD

Contents

PART 2
BETWEEN VOICES: INTERVIEWS

PART 3
APPENDICES

About the author

Kintto Lucas, a Uruguayan, is a journalist, editor and poet who has been living and working in Ecuador since 1992 where he has been culture editor and columnist on the daily *Hoy*, and editor of the magazine *Chasqui*. Books include:

Treinta poemas de amor y vida, (ed), Tché, Montevideo, 1986.
Caminamundos, (ed) Tierradentro, Montevideo 1988.
Fantasmas, (ed) Tierradentro, Montevideo, 1990.
Rebeliones Indígenas y Negras en América Latina – Entre viento y fuego, (ed), Abya Yala, Quito, 1992, 1993, 1997.
Desmadre de tiempo y geografías, (ed), CEQUIPUS, Quito, 1993.
Diario de viaje – conociendo el país, (ed), CIESPAL, Quito 1994.
Antología de editoriales del diario HOY 1994, (co-author), Edimpres, Quito, 1995.
Antología de editoriales del diario HOY 1995, (co-author), Edimpres, Quito, 1996.
Mujeres del siglo XX, (ed) Abya Yala, Quito, 1997, 1998, 1999.
La sed y el agua, (ed) Abya Yala, 1997.
Antología de cuentos sobre mujeres, (co-author) París, 1997.
Apuntes sobre fútbol, (ed) Abya Yala, 1998.
Actores de cambio en América Latina, (co-author) Latinamerica Press, 1999
La rebelión de los indios, Abya Yala, Quito, 2000, Nordam Editorial, Montevideo, 2000.

Kintto Lucas was awarded the José Martí Prize for Journalism in Latin American in 1990.

Editor's note

La Rebelión de los Indios was published in Ecuador a matter of weeks after the January 2000 *levantamiento indígena* (indigenous uprising), at the end of a particularly tumultuous chapter in the country's recent history. A collection of news, feature articles and interviews written between March 1999 and January 2000, at one level it offers a blow-by-blow account of the march on the capital Quito by thousands of indigenous, and of the unravelling of the presidency of Jamil Mahuad. At another level it provides a snapshot of economic, environmental and social conditions facing the people of Ecuador today. The combined effect is a rare insight into the profound changes affecting this under-reported country.

In editing we have tried to preserve the meaning and texture of the original while eliminating the sort of repetition that is characteristic of rolling news coverage. Some material did not appear in the original Spanish: notes and glosses were added (mostly by the author) in May 2000 as were the bibliography and list of contacts; the map, socio-economic statistics, and Appendices 1 and 2 were added by CIIR.

Not all opinions expressed in what follows necessarily reflect any agreed policy of CIIR, its members or trustees.

Adam Bradbury, CIIR
June 2000

INTRODUCTION

MAURICIO USHIÑA

We come from yesterday bringing memories of rebels and rebellions. We return to the present to walk the corners of Ecuador, be with its people and travel with them...500 years later.

FROM RUMIÑAHUI TO CONAIE

1

The history of the Ecuadorian indigenous movement goes back to the first rebellions against the conquest. Here we find Rumiñahui who led the resistance against the Spanish invasion in 1535, and Jumandi who headed the rebellion of the natives of Amazonia in 1578.[1] We remember Daquilema, who in the republican period in 1871 initiated the uprising of the province of Chimborazo, in the central Sierra, against the conservative government of Gabriel García Moreno.[2] But it is in the 20th century that the indigenous people from different regions of Ecuador begin to join together. In the early decades of this century we find women such as Dolores Cacuango and Tránsito Amaguaña. The latter created the first agricultural trade union in the country, led the first indigenous peasant strike in 1944, helped to found the Ecuadorian Federation of Indians and set up peasant schools, where teaching was conducted in

[1] **Rumiñahui** was the warrior brother of the king of the Incas, Atahualpa. Unlike his brother, Rumiñahui decided not to capitulate to the *conquistador*, Francisco Pizarro. He was driven back to Quito, from where he fought off Pedro de Alvarado, the *conquistador* of Guatemala, and it was said that 'nobody defeats the lord of Quito'. Sebastián de Benalcazar, the founder of Guayaquil, was given the task of finding him. After intense battles and much resistence Rumiñahui was captured and tortured to get him to reveal where he had hidden the treasures of Atahualpa. Rumiñahui deceived them about the whereabouts of the treasure, in return for which Benalcazar had him burnt at the stake. **Jumandi** was the great king of the Amazonian Quijos. He and his high priests attacked the Spanish towns of Avila and Archidona. After their victory Jumandi took charge of the liberation of the Quijos and decided to attack firstly Baeza and later Quito. He is said to have exhorted highland indians to join the uprising with the words: 'The expulsion of the invaders must be total. Our suffering is the same as our brothers in the mountains. The freedom of the Quijos starts with the freedom of us all.' When Jumandi and the high priests were defeated, they were taken to Quito where they were hung, drawn and quartered and their heads left displayed in the main square for many years.

[2] Gabriel García Moreno held power from 1860 until he was assassinated in 1875. Supported by estate-owners in the Sierra, he attempted to centralise power and tax collection, and turned Ecuador into an ultra-conservative Catholic state. Today the Catholic church still carries enormous weight in Ecuador, claiming more than 90 per cent of the population. However, the number is decreasing in favour of envangelical sects (Roos, 1997).

Quechua for the first time. For this 'audacity' she was persecuted and imprisoned.

Another half-century was to pass before the indigenous movement had any real impact on national life again. In June 1990 the indigenous joined together in the Confederation of Indigenous Nations of Ecuador (CONAIE)[3] for the greatest uprising. They occupied roads, invaded *latifundios* (large estates)[4] detained soldiers, withheld products from the market, took over public offices, and organised marches and demonstrations. With the army

immediately taking to the streets, there were confrontations. They beat people up and used their guns to defend landholders, even though the social-democratic president, Rodrigo Borja, favoured dialogue.[5]

The 1990 uprising was to become symbolic of the indigenous peoples' breakthrough into modern politics. But it also caused an upheaval within the army. A closer relationship developed between the army and indigenous people as officers and men with links in the community engaged in social work.

In October 1992, with the slogan

---

[3] The Confederation of Indigenous Nations of Ecuador (CONAIE) was formed in 1986 among the different indigenous peoples, who wanted a forum that would unite them without going through political parties and organisations. At first it addressed ethnic and cultural issues, but over time made the transition into national politics. With some 26 affiliated organisations CONAIE represents all the indigenous nations of Ecuador – Awa, Chachi, Epera, Tsáchila, Cofán, Siona, Secoya, Huaorani, Achaur, Shuar and all the peoples of the Quechua nation – Natabuelas, Otavalos, Caranquis, Cayambis, Quitus, Panzaleos, Salasacas, Chibuleos, Puruhaes, Warankas, Cañaris and Saraguros – which is the best organised and most numerous, with more than 3 million people. CONAIE emerged into public life during the 1990 *levantamiento indígena*, which was triggered by the granting of oil concessions in indigenous territories to foreign companies. CONAIE's directors are elected every two years in a congress which brings together more than 1,000 delegates from the different communities. Most nations are represented among the directors, who have executive power, but every two months receive instructions from CONAIE's 100-member assembly.

[4] *Latifundios* are large farming estates. A tiny percentage of farms own a substantial proportion of productive farmland (in the Sierra less than 2 per cent of farms accounted for 43 per cent of land in 1994). A land reform programme between the 1960s and 1980s saw 1.8 million acres shared out among 95,000 families, but many of the original plots

have since been subdivided, and peasant holdings tend to be on land that is poorly irrigated, and vulnerable to erosion by rain and over-cultivation. As soil becomes unproductive small-scale farmers tend to move to ever-steeper slopes on higher ground, where harvests are even less reliable and where a fragile eco-system is increasingly under threat. Many peasants still work as labourers on *latifundios*, although many menfolk migrate to the cities in search of work.

[5] Rodrigo Borja Cevallos, president of Ecuador 1988-92. He succeeded León Febres Cordero (1984-88), whose presidency was marked by systematic violation of human rights. Borja founded the social-democratic Izquierda Democrática (ID – Democratic Left; see Table 3, page 15, for political parties). Borja broke with the previous government's neo-liberal zeal and proposed a programme of social-democratic reforms, opposed privatisation of state companies, and began to dismantle the repressive apparatus created under Febres Cordero. His reform programme was stymied by soaring inflation and political deadlock between the labour movement and industrialists.

'We will not dance on our grandparents' tombs', indigenous people from across the country marched to Quito to commemorate the '500 years of indigenous resistance'.[6]

From then on, the indigenous movement became the most important social movement in Ecuador and one of the best-organised in Latin America. It was the only one capable of paralysing the country, and became a feature of politics in Ecuador that could no longer be ignored. Miguel Lluco, a leading indigenous figure, says: 'Ecuador's plural nature is demonstrated when the indigenous emerge as a protagonist in socio-political life. Then it is recognised that the "other" exists and they have their differences and their rights' (see interview with Miguel Lluco, page 112).

2

The ability to mobilise, and the growing influence of the indigenous movement in non-indigenous sectors, gave rise to the idea of participating in elections. Discussions on the subject lasted for more than a year between 1995 and 1996. Some within the movement wanted to transform CONAIE into a political party. Others opposed becoming involved in elections on the grounds that this might blur the role of the indigenous movement and divert it from its central struggle, which was working to organise communities, land occupations, the recovery of cultural and ethnic identities, and uprisings as a form of protest.

It was eventually decided that the movement should take part in the electoral process through an organisational structure that would demonstrate the alliance of the indigenous sectors with other social movements in both rural and urban areas.

For the elections of 1996 this resulted in the birth of Movimiento de Unidad Plurinacional Pachakutik – País Nuevo (PN – Pachakutik Movement for Pluri-national Unity – New Country), to field candidates at local level and to provincial councils. Later, social organisations and the indigenous communities themselves decided to field candidates for the national parliament (until 1998 the single-chamber parliament included provincial representatives who sat for two years, and national representatives who, like the president, sat for four years). To do this they also had to take part in the presidential election. As the movement was not a political party, in order to comply with the electoral requirements and field national candidates, the indigenous movement had to present 100,000 signatures.

The candidates were named after a long assembly, and the signatures were gathered in one week, which was unprecedented in Ecuador. The social organisations put forward as their presidential candidate the journalist Fredy Ehlers, whose career had always been linked to progressive sectors. As their first candidate for the national parliament, they put forward the indigenous Quechua, Luis Macas, who had a long record of social struggles. He was one of the founders of CONAIE and its president at the time (see interview, page 104).

When asked why the indigenous movement was taking part in the elections, Macas said that it was just another form of struggle. 'The organisations have various ways of fighting for their claims,' he argued. 'There are uprisings, which we resort to when necessary; there is bilingual education in Quechua and Spanish to save our language; and the elections are just another form of struggle. Until

[6] The phrase 'We will not dance on our grandparents' tombs' captured the sentiment of the indigenous movement when Spain and other countries were preparing to celebrate the 500th anniversary of the Conquest, in 1992. The indigenous declared that the date really marked 500 years of resistance to a culture which for centuries had sought to dominate them.

now we did not see the need to take part in elections, because we did not have the processes in place. Now we are facing the challenge.'

Macas explains that the essence of Pachakutik is unity in diversity. 'In it there are urban workers, non-indigenous peasants, ecologists, Afro-Ecuadorians, and indigenous.'

In the elections Ehlers came third after the populist Abdalá Bucaram and the right-winger, Jaime Nebot. Macas succeeded in combining the indigenous vote – a sector which did not generally vote at all because the indigenous did not feel represented – with the vote of progressive and left-wing sectors in the towns. His electoral campaign canvassed communities and districts door-to-door. Financial difficulties prevented Pachakutik from campaigning on television and the party opted instead for radio publicity. Nevertheless, Pachakutik won 10 per cent of the vote.

Elected president in the second round, Abdalá Bucaram embarked on a policy that was intended to break up the indigenous movement. He offered jobs and money to some regional leaders, which provoked an immediate reaction from CONAIE. The organisation's member of parliament Miguel Lluco, together with other popular leaders, occupied Quito Cathedral in an action which signalled the beginning of the end for Bucaram.

At the end of 1996, a National Constituent Assembly to Reform the Ecuadorian Constitution summoned back the indigenous and social movements.[7] While the campaign to elect assembly members was going on, 10,000 indigenous from all over the country marched on Quito to set up the Popular Constituent Assembly, together with other social sectors. This Assembly had the task of working out an alternative constitutional plan

ASSOCIATED PRESS

which would be accepted by the representatives of Pachakutik.

[7] Ecuador had 19 different constitutions between 1830 and 1979. The 1979 constitution re-established civilian democracy after years of military rule and provided for a single chamber parliament – the congress – and an executive led by a popularly elected president. During the 1980s the president was rarely able to count on a majority in congress. In 1998 the popularly constituted National Constituent Assembly – comprising 70 representatives including seven from the Pachakutik movement – introduced a series of constitutional reforms intended to tip the balance of power away from congress and towards the executive, and improve governability and political continuity. Reforms included abolishing mid-term congressional elections and stripping congress of its power to impeach ministers. The number of members of parliament was raised from 82 to 121 in order to strengthen representation of densely populated districts. For the Political Constitution of the Republic of Ecuador, see www.ecuanex.net. ec/constitucion/index.html

ECUADOR

Ecuador covers an area of 283,561 square km on South America's Pacific coast. To the north it shares a border with Colombia, and to the east and south with Peru. The sovereignty of some 200,000 square km of Amazon rainforest to Ecuador's east – an area almost as large as Ecuador again – was for more than 50 years the subject of dispute between Ecuador and Peru that occasionally led to outbreaks of fighting between the two countries. Ecuador never recognised the 1942 Rio de Janeiro Protocol delineating its border with Peru. The most recent conflict occurred in January 1995 in the remote Cordillera del Cóndor in southern Ecuador. In a month's fighting about 100 soldiers were killed. The long-running dispute was finally brought to an end in 1998 when president Jamil Mahuad of Ecuador and Peru's Alberto Fujimori signed a permanent agreement defining a border and awarding Ecuador unlimited (though not sovereign) navigation rights on the Amazon river.

Ecuador's environment, patterns of habitation and land use are determined by its three distinct geographical regions – coast, highlands and Amazon rainforest. The high plateau, or Sierra, between two ranges of the Andes allows for the growth of subsistence crops and livestock farming, and is the area with the highest population density. However, more than half the country's population lives along the coast, where, despite its proximity to the Equator, the climate is moderated by the cold Humboldt current. Cash crops of bananas, cocoa, rice, coffee and shrimp are produced along the coast.

The diversity of Ecuador's natural habitats (including the Galápagos Islands) makes it one of the most species-rich countries on the planet, and this is a major draw for tourism, Ecuador's fourth-largest foreign exchange earner. Yet Ecuador's habitats and many unique species are under threat. Deforestation is a severe problem in all three natural zones. On the coast shrimp farming in particular has seen the destruction of enormous areas of mangrove forest to make way for artificial ponds. Some 95 per cent of forest in the Sierra and on western lowlands and slopes of the Andes have disappeared. The Amazon rainforest is coming under increasing threat from cattle-ranching, logging and oil extraction. The latter has also led to problems with pollution as toxic waste products have been released into the water system.

ESTIMATED INDIGENOUS POPULATION OF ECUADOR

Pacific coast		Amazon basin	
Awa	1,600	Quechua	60,000
Chachi	4,000	Cofán	800
Tsáchila	2,000	Siona-Secoya	1,000
		Shuar	40,000
Sierra highlands		Achuar	500
Quechua	3 million	Huaorani	2,000

Sources: *Ecuador in Focus. A Guide to the People, Politics and Culture*, Latin America Bureau, London 1997; *Ecuador Country Profile 1999-2000*, Economist Intelligence Unit, London 1999; website of CONAIE: www.conaie.nativeweb.org.

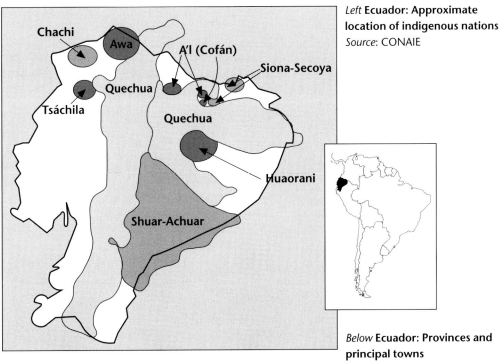

Left **Ecuador: Approximate location of indigenous nations**
Source: CONAIE

Below **Ecuador: Provinces and principal towns**

3

Some 3.5 million of Ecuador's 11.5 million inhabitants are indigenous, grouped into 11 nations. Most of them live in rural areas. The largest nation is Quechua, who live in the Sierra region and Amazonia or Oriente. The Awa, Chachi, Epera, and Tsáchila nations live on the Pacific Ocean coast. The Cofán, Siona, Secoya, Huaorani, Achuar, and Shuar live in Amazonia.

The indigenous adhere to a value system handed down over generations. Miguel Lluco, a Quechua, champions a model of community and solidarity that has been practiced for hundreds of years: when a family in the community is in a difficult situation, everybody joins together to help. As well as this, there is *minga*, communal work to build a road or a house or for the harvest. 'That's why we say that our movement is in "*minga* for life," [ie working in common for the sake of life],' says Lluco.

In terms of electoral experience, he points to the management of town halls. 'We have the municipal assemblies, where community representatives analyse the budget, set spending priorities, and control and keep track of investments.'

Ecuador's new constitution recognises the collective rights of different peoples and the pluri-ethnic and multi-cultural character of the country.[8] In addition Agreement 169 of the International Labour Organisation (ILO) has been approved, recognising the rights of indigenous peoples.[9] It was Lluco who saw the approval of Agreement 169 through parliament. 'The basic principles of the agreement are respect for the traditional cultures, ways of life and forms of organisation of our peoples and their effective participation in decisions that affect them,' he says.

'According to Agreement 169, judges in ordinary courts who deal with offences committed by indigenous have a duty to take account of indigenous norms, customs and culture as mitigating factors when it comes to sentencing,' he says.

It is also recognised that indigenous peoples can exercise judicial functions, through their own authorities, in order to resolve conflicts and administer justice in accordance with their communal tradition. 'It is necessary to harmonise the laws and establish levels of competence so that indigenous and national laws do not clash or contradict each other,' Lluco says.

The official use of indigenous languages is also recognised. If an indigenous person has to make an application in a public office and does not speak Spanish, the officials must attend to him in his own language. 'We have had advances in cultural and political matters, but we are still behind economically. In its commitment to plurality, the state should redirect public funds towards the economy of the popular sectors and indigenous peoples,' says Lluco.

Pachakutik is to the left of the political spectrum. But Lluco makes it clear that the organisation has nothing to do with the traditional left, which always looked abroad and did

[8] The reformed constitution recognised the collective rights of indigenous peoples, and respect for their ancestral practices in areas such as medicine and justice. It declared Ecuador a multi-cultural and pluri-ethnic country but stopped short of accepting the indigenous proposal that it be a pluri-national country. By May 2000 none of these advances had been translated from paper into practice because congress had not yet passed the necessary implementing legislation.

[9] For extracts of ILO 169, see Appendix 2, page 124.

not understand the indigenous movement. 'We are peoples struggling to consolidate a different agenda, which is the construction of the pluri-national state,' he says.

The demand that Ecuador should be pluri-national has been interpreted by some sectors as its geographical division into various states. Lluco says that the pluri-national state is a single state with juridical plurality in the territories inhabited by indigenous nations, and their right to decide for themselves politically, economically, culturally and socially. 'The national territory is not dismembered but our peoples are accorded further levels of decision-making and autonomy, as laid down by Agreement 169,' he says.

4

In 1998 the Popular Democratic (Christian democrat) Jamil Mahuad was elected president of Ecuador.

Pachakutik gained six seats in parliament, and the indigenous member, Nina Pacari, was appointed vice-president of the chamber (see interview with Nina Pacari, page 108).

Between November 1998 and February 1999 five banks crashed and the state took over their debts, disbursing more than US$1.5 billion. In March 1999 the Progress Bank, the largest on the coast, ran into liquidity problems. As the government had no money to save it, and under pressure from Guayaquil-based finance groups, Jamil Mahuad decreed a bank holiday for a week. He ordered a fuel price rise and froze for one year deposits in current and savings accounts containing more than US$200. The indigenous movement joined with the taxi drivers to bring the country to a standstill, and Mahuad retreated on the fuel price rise.

QUITO AND GUAYAQUIL

Ecaudor's history has been dominated by the antagonism and struggle for supremacy between its two major cities, Quito and Guayaquil. Once divided into four autonomous regions, in 1869 Ecuador began to consolidate as a single state. But a history of neglect of the regions by the cetre has led to growing discontent and increasing interest in regional autonomy.

The province of Guayas is situated in the coastal region, on the Pacific Ocean, and its capital is the port of Guayaquil. Although Quito, in the Sierra, is the official political centre, Guayaquil has the largest population and is the country's chief commercial centre. It is also the city with the largest gap between rich and poor and with the worst urban violence.

Economic and political groups in Guayaquil are pushing for autonomy for the province. Following the collapse of the Progress Bank in March 1999, up to 50,000 people took to the streets to demonstrate for autonomy. The principal shareholder, Fernando Aspiazu, and the mayor of Guayaquil, León Febres Cordero, blamed the bank's collapse on Quito's centralism.

They claimed that the bank had been damaged by the Mahuad government's preference for depositing public funds in the Sierra banks. They demanded that the authorities provide assistance to save the Progress Bank. The Guayaquil Chambers of Industry and Commerce joined them in their demand and also demanded, as part of 'better treatment' for the region, that they should not be charged income tax or capital gains tax. Some analysts say the Guayaquil businessmen and the Christian Social Party are using regionalism as a way of imposing their desire for an economic model that favours them.

In January 2000, a week after the uprising of the indigenous peoples and the colonels, 95 per cent of the population of the province of Guayas voted in favour of autonomy for the province in a regional plebiscite. There are growing demands that the income generated in the province should remain in the province. The tensions between Guayaquil and Quito, which are echoed in the loyalties of the armed forces, could contribute to a 'Balkanisation' of the country and the possibility of armed civil conflict.

But the crisis deepened and in July 1999, after a further rise in fuel prices, the indigenous staged another uprising together with taxi drivers and other sectors. More than 15,000 indigenous arrived in Quito to demand that the measures be reviewed. After a big demonstration in the capital and 10 hours of talks between the president and 50 indigenous – including the indigenous leaders Antonio Vargas (see interview with Antonio Vargas, page 100) and Ricardo Ulcuango and the peasant leader Jorge Loor – CONAIE again achieved its objectives: the president retreated on the price rises and accelerated the unfreezing of deposits retained in March.

'We have demonstrated the strength in the unity of indigenous nations, together with peasants, trades unions and popular urban organisations,' Ulcuango said. 'The people do not rise every three months. When they do they must be listened to. When they protest against anti-popular measures, like those introduced by the present government, what they have to say must be respected,' says Lluco.

5

Parallel with the deepening of the economic crisis and the resurgence of the indigenous, from early 1999 there was growing discontent among progressive officers in the army demanding action to put an end to the corruption of bankers. They called for imprisonment for the corrupt bankers who were still in the country and the extradition of those who had fled abroad. The government and the military authorities ignored the officers' demands. This created a general discontent and fostered rebellion.

With his popularity rating at barely 8 per cent, Mahuad tried a change of tactics to unite the right, businessmen, bankers and the mainstream media. On 9 January 2000 he announced the dollarisation of the Ecuadorian economy. This was the last straw and turned both indigenous and military against the government. On 10 and 11 January CONAIE, together with other social movements, set up 'popular parliaments' in every province and the National Parliament of the Peoples of Ecuador in Quito. On 15 January the indigenous and popular uprising began calling for the dissolution of the three powers of the state – the executive, legislature and judiciary. The officers issued an ultimatum to the military authorities, and from there to insurrection was a single step. The uprising started on Friday 21 January with the taking of parliament by the indigenous, supported by army officers rebelling against the government.

On the following day, leaders of the civic-military insurrection installed a Junta of National Salvation, consisting of colonel Lucio Gutiérrez, Antonio Vargas, president of CONAIE, and the former president of the supreme court of justice, Carlos Solórzano. They

LORI WASELCHUK

Soldiers and civilians on the Panamerican Highway, January 2000.

repudiated the three powers of the State. In the afternoon, general Carlos Mendoza, chief of the joint command of the armed forces, demanded the resignation of Jamil Mahuad so that military chiefs could be installed in his place. Mahuad abandoned the government palace.

That night, the members of the junta marched to the seat of government accompanied by thousands of demonstrators to hold talks with Mendoza, who still controlled most military units. The insurgents had the support of part of the army, the indigenous movement and the social organisations, who continued their protests on the streets, with occupations of government offices and public buildings in provinces across the country.

At one o'clock in the morning on

Saturday 22 January, the military authorities reached an agreement with the insurgents, which resulted in Mendoza becoming a member of the junta. Three hours later Mendoza, together with the military high command, carried out a coup to enable the vice- president Gustavo Noboa to take over the presidency.

'Mendoza betrayed the indigenous and popular movement and placed himself at the service of the corrupt people who govern this country,' said Vargas. 'After undertaking to respect the will of the people, who were on the streets demanding an end to deals with corrupt bankers and the usual politicians, Mendoza retreated and sullied his military uniform. But we indigenous will stay mobilised and continue to be vigilant,' he added.

Colonel Gutiérrez was arrested early on the Saturday morning by people in civilian clothes, who said they belonged to the armed forces intelligence service. The colonel's wife, Ximena Bohoquez, told the media that she was afraid for his life. In the hours that followed, other officers were arrested and placed under the order of the military court. Finance minister, Mariana Yepez, asked the president of

the supreme court, Galo Pico, to initiate proceedings and decree the preventive imprisonment of Antonio Vargas, Carlos Solórzano, and members of parliament, Paco Moncayo and René Yandún,[10] for their part in the rebellion.

The president of CONAIE said the indigenous uprising had not been a disaster because it had confirmed their organisational strength and power to mobilise. 'We have demonstrated that we are a force. We will learn various lessons from this insurrection, so that we do not make the same mistake of believing in traitors like the military authorities,' he said.

He said that the unity and patience of the indigenous movement demonstrated that it was possible to conduct a entirely peaceful uprising in order to secure changes. He asked the supreme court to inform him when he should present himself at the prison. 'Here I am. I am not going to run away, because I am not a banker, or a businessman, not one of those who rob money from the people and run off to the United States,' he said. The leader argued that if they were going to imprison all those who had taken part, they would have to build gigantic prisons, 'because there are millions of us in the country and in the towns'.

Luis Macas (see interview, page 104) insists that nothing will prevent the indigenous Ecuadorians from continuing to build up their power. 'Ushay, the Quechua word for power, means improving living conditions. It is our capacity to develop collectively, and make our own contributions from where we stand,' he said while he watched his brothers and sisters beginning their march back to their communities. But history does not end. It begins again, and again. The same fire impels it to begin yet again.

---

[10] **Paco Moncayo** commands national respect for his conduct, as head of the joint chiefs of staff, of the conflict against Peru in the Cordillera del Cóndor. In May 2000 he was elected mayor of Quito on a ticket representing ID, Pachakutik, the Movimiento Popular Democrático (MPD, Popular Democratic Movement) and the Partido Socialista Ecuatoriano (PSE, Ecuadorian Socialist Party). **René Yandún**, an army general closely linked to the peasant sector, spoke out against corruption during the interim presidency of Fabian Alarcón (1997-98). Elected to congress as a deputy for the ID, both he and Moncayo were removed by the majority right wing after supporting the January 2000 *levantamiento indígena.*

TABLE 1: ECUADOR IN FIGURES

		Date	Source
POPULATION			
Total population	12.6 million	2000 (estimate)	Third World Guide
Population growth rate	2.3% per year	1998	INEC, BCE
Urban population	59.6%	1996	Third World Guide
Guayaquil	1.87 million	1995	Third World Guide
Quito	1.4 million	1995	Third World Guide
Cuenca	0.33 million	1995	Third World Guide
Mestizo (mixed Hispanic and indigenous)	55%	1999	World Fact Book
Indigenous	25%	1999	World Fact Book
Spanish	10%	1999	World Fact Book
Afro-Ecuadorian	10%	1999	World Fact Book
POVERTY			
Percentage of population below poverty line	35%	1994	World Fact Book
LABOUR FORCE			
Area of employment (% of total)			
Agriculture	29	1990	World Fact Book
Manufacturing	18	1990	World Fact Book
Commerce	15	1990	World Fact Book
Other	38	1990	World Fact Book
URBAN LABOUR FORCE			
Male	60.9%	1999	INEC
Female	39.1%	1999	INEC
Unemployed	9.2%	1999	INEC
Under-employed	40.4%	1999	INEC
Economically active population	3.4 million	1999	INEC
HEALTH			
Life expectancy at birth	70 years (male)	1996	Third World Guide
Life expectancy at birth	67 years (female)	1994	Third World Guide
Infant mortality	31 per 1,000	1996	Third World Guide
Under-five child mortality	40 per 1,000	1996	Third World Guide
No. of children per woman	3.2	1996	Third World Guide
LITERACY			
Male	90%	1995	Third World Guide
Female	88%	1995	Third World Guide

		Date	Source
ECONOMY			
Gross domestic product			
GDP	US$19.7 billion	1998	BCE, IMF
GDP growth	0.4% per year	1998	BCE, IMF
GDP by sector (% of total)			
Agriculture, forestry, fishing	18	1998	BCE
Oil and mining	14.2	1998	BCE
Manufacturing	16.3	1998	BCE
Trade, tourism	15.9	1998	BCE
Finance, business, services	8.1	1998	BCE
Inflation	36% per year	1998	BCE
Exports (US$ million)			
Oil and derivatives	925	1998	BCE
Bananas, plantains	1,070	1998	BCE
Shrimp	872	1998	BCE
Coffee and derivatives	105	1998	BCE
Food import dependency	5%	1994	Third World Guide
Debt (US$ billion)			
Public (medium and long-term)	12.376	1997	World Bank
Private (medium and long term)	0.340	1997	World Bank
Total external debt	14.918	1997	World Bank

Sources: Instituto Nacional de Estadística y Censos (INEC), Banco Central de Ecuador (BCE), International Monetary Fund (IMF), World Bank cited in Economist Intelligence Unit, *Ecuador Country Profile 1999-2000*; CIA World Fact Book.

TABLE 2: ECUADOR: ECONOMIC COMPARISONS WITH OTHER COUNTRIES, 1998

	Ecuador	Colombia	Peru	United States	Chile
GDP (US$ billion)	19.7	94.0	62.4	8,759.9	73.0
GDP per head (US$)	1,708	2,297	2,517	32,409	4,922
Consumer price inflation (average % per year)	36.0	20.4	7.3	1.6	5.3
Current account balance as % of GDP	−10.2	−6.2	−6.1	−2.5	−5.7
External debt (US$ billion)	15.3	34.7	30.6	37.8	N/A
Debt-service ratio, paid (%)	36.3	34.2	34.2	21.5	N/A

Source: BCE, IMF, EIU CountryData cited in Economist Intelligence Unit *Ecuador Country Profile, 1999-2000*.

TABLE 3: ECUADOR'S POLITICAL PARTIES, 1999

Acronym	Name	No. of seats in parliament (1999)	Character
PSC	Partido Social Cristiano	27	Centre-right. Led by León Febres Cordero (president 1984-98; mayor of Guayaquil 1992-96 and 1996-2000); and by Jaime Nebot, elected Mayor of Guayaquil in May 2000.
PCE	Partido Conservativo Ecuatoriano	3	Centre-right.
ID	Izquierda Democrática	18	Centre-left. Social-democratic party affiliated to international socialist movement. One of its most important figures Rodrigo Borja Cevallos was president, 1988-92.
DP	Democrácia Popular	32	In the 1980s DP was of the centre but during the government of Jamil Mahuad (mayor of Quito 1992-96 and 1996-98; president 1998-2000) moved to the right, allying itself with the PSC. Formerly Democrácia Cristiana, governed 1980-84. Vice-president Osvaldo Hurtado took over presidency on the death of Jaime Roldós Aguilera in an air crash that some people think was organised by the CIA for his support for the Sandinistas in Nicaragua.
FRA	Frente Radical Alfarista	5	Centre-left
PRE	Partido Roldosista Ecuatoriano	24	Populist-right. Led by Abdalá Bucaram who was dismissed from the presidency in 1997 on charges of corruption. It is strongest in the coastal provinces.
CFP	Concentración de Fuerzas Populares	1	Populist
PN	Movimiento Pachakutik–País Nuevo	9	Political expression of the indigenous and other social movements.
MPD	Movimiento Popular Democrático	2	Left/Marxist. Assassination of leader Jaime Hurtado in 1998 has been linked to the police.
	Various	10	Independents

Source: Political Database of the Americas/OAS, CIA World Fact Book, Economist Intelligence Unit *Ecuador Country Profile 1999-2000*.

PART 1

BETWEEN FIRES: CHRONICLE OF THE UPRISINGS

March 1999 - January 2000

Fire leaps up brightly, within set confines. But sometimes, as it advances along the road of time, it becomes diffuse. The flames turn from yellow to red, and the red may become blue. Then the fire, which seemed to have meaning, remains untended and dies down. Yet fire can be part of the rainbow and assume all its colours. Now, 10 years after the uprising that revived the fire with its seven colours, it is worth looking again, not at the magic of its appearance, but its meaning and take that as a way forward.[11]

[11] The *huípala*, comprising the seven colours of the rainbow, is an indigenous symbol and the flag of unity among the communities. The seven colours signify the unity of the indigenous against the Conquest and are a sign of new times, new life, the new *pachakutik*, a period which comes every 100 years and revives indigenous culture and justice. The Pachakutik Movement adopted the *huípala* as its symbol. Fire represents the power of collective organisation, the 'heat of community'.

Progress on ice

14 March 1999 (Saturday) Ecuador has been through four days of uncertainty this week – a bank holiday, a state of national emergency, a two-day general strike and the announcement of new economic measures.

In less than two months, five banks have crashed and the state has taken over their debts, disbursing more than US$1.5 billion. On 8 March, the Progress Bank, the biggest on the coast, ran into liquidity problems. The value of the US currency rose by 100 per cent, as had happened the week before.

Fearing further strengthening of the dollar, and under pressure from the Guayaquil finance groups to save the bank, Jamil Mahuad declared a bank holiday and announced that on 11 March he would publish new economic measures to mitigate the crisis. The news only intensified doubts about the country's economic and political stability. Rumours arose of a possible coup as a political solution, and convertibility or dollarisation as an economic solution. The uncertainty deepened when the president decided to extend the bank holiday until 9 March and decreed a state of national emergency, prohibiting any protest.

On 10 March a 48-hour general strike began, called by social and trades union organisations and the indigenous movement. It was supported by opposition parties. Ecuador's major cities remained paralysed throughout 10 and 11 March. The strikers organised protest marches which were repressed, leading to confrontations with the police. Indigenous people closed roads in the mountain areas.

The Coordinating Committee of Social Movements, the Confederation of Indigenous Nations of Ecuador (CONAIE), the United Workers' Front, human rights organisations and the left and centre-left parties convened a people's congress, which was attended by 3,000 people on 11 March. The congress put forward a proposal to end the economic crisis. It proposed the restoration of income tax; the removal of value-added tax (VAT) exemptions except for food and medicine; and the imposition of a progressive tax on luxury private cars, aeroplanes and private yachts. It also proposed the removal of customs exemptions, the rationalisation of public spending and a suspension in the servicing of foreign debt.

That night, the president announced the government's measures, stressing that 'the great battle we must fight is against hyperinflation'. Fuel prices rose by 163 per cent. Mahuad also announced the urgent introduction of 12 new bills into parliament. One of these increased VAT from 10 to 15 per cent and set a tax on cars valued at more than US$15,000. 'It is better to raise a tax than for the dollar to triple,' Mahuad said.

He said parliament would also deal urgently with other bills proposed by the executive to smooth the way for the immediate privatisation of the telephone, electricity, oil, ports and the post office. The bank holiday was extended until the Monday. To prevent a massive withdrawal of money the government froze deposits in current accounts, savings and fixed term accounts, in *sucres*[12] and dollars. It prohibited the withdrawal for a year of 50 per cent of credit balances in excess of US$200, and prohibited any withdrawal of foreign currency deposits in excess of US$500.

Mahuad stated that this economic

[12] Ecuadorian currency, named after field marshal Antonio José de Sucre, the hero of Ecuador's independence from Spain. One of Simon Bolivar's officers, de Sucre defeated the Spanish at the Battle of Pichincha (1822) and took Quito.

package 'would establish the basis to implement future convertibility or directly to dollarise the Ecuadorian economy'.

Former president Rodrigo Borja, a social democrat, disagreed with Mahuad's plan and said: 'You can't fight inflation by raising the price of fuel by 100 per cent and maintaining an unfunded budget.'

Miguel Lluco, the indigenous leader, and the national coordinating committee of the Movimiento de Unidad Plurinacional Pachakutik – País Nuevo (MUPP-PN, Pachakutik Movement for Pluri-national Unity – New Country, the political arm of the indigenous and social movements), said the measures were an attack on the middle class and the poor. 'It freezes deposits from US$150 upwards, affecting those who have least. It raises fuel prices leading to a rise in the prices of basic necessities. It bails out the banks, even though the fiscal deficit is largely due to them,' Lluco said.

The social and indigenous organisations called for civil disobedience and announced protest demonstrations and road blocks. They also threatened an indefinite strike.

The day after he proclaimed his measures, Mahuad's popularity plummeted. In six months it has fallen by 52 points; from 66 percent when he took over the government to 14 per cent today.

16 March 1999 (Tuesday) Lorry and bus drivers blocked Ecuador's roads when they joined the strike started yesterday by taxi drivers, who have cut off the streets of the capital in protest against the rise in petrol prices.

This coming Wednesday an indigenous uprising will also begin. Thousands of people will take over the country's roads and stop agricultural produce reaching the market. As on other occasions, this could cause the cities to go short of supplies.

Last Thursday president Jamil Mahuad set out a new economic package, in which the two key measures were a fuel price rise of 163 per cent and the freezing of bank deposits.

Taxi drivers' leader Pedro Alava said: 'We can't work with petrol at that price. If we put up our fares, people won't pay them. This affects us and so does the rise of the dollar. Many of us went into debt to buy new taxis with the dollar at 6,500 *sucres* and within three months it had gone up to 11,000.'

Since yesterday the people of Quito have had to get to work on foot or by bicycle. Buses and private cars have been unable to run because of the blockade mounted by the capital's 9,000 taxi drivers. Traffic was also jammed in other cities.

The government ordered the armed forces to remove the taxis from the streets under the state of national emergency in force since last week. Defence minister general José Gallardo accused the taxi drivers of causing chaos and anarchy. 'This will not be permitted by the armed forces, who will be put in charge of maintaining order,' he said.

The taxi drivers' protest began a week in which various social sectors called for 'civil disobedience' to demand a government revision of some of the economic measures. 'We offered proposals to deal with the crisis to members of the government and economic ministers, but they did not take any notice,' said Antonio Vargas, president of CONAIE.

The indigenous movement in Ecuador is the social sector with the greatest capacity for mobilisation. Sixty per cent of agricultural production is grown on indigenous communities' small plots of land. 'We are obliged to take a stand against economic measures that only hit the poor. Our opinions do not matter to the government, but the indigenous nations and social movements continue to be open to dialogue,' said Vargas.

Finance minister Ana Lucía Armijos said: 'The measures are not going to be revised, because they are fundamental to overcoming the crisis.' But she insisted: 'The government has always been open to dialogue.'

Rumours persist that the executive is about to dissolve parliament. However, the government called an urgent meeting with opposition leaders to ask for their proposals for overcoming the crisis. General Paco Moncayo, former chief of the joint command of the armed forces, and currently a member of parliament for the social-democratic Democratic Left, appreciated the government's approach to dialogue with the opposition. Moncayo demanded an immediate end to the state of emergency and a cut in fuel prices in order to restore calm, which would make it possible to implement alternative measures to get the country out of the crisis.

18 March 1999 (Thursday) President Jamil Mahuad has promised to end the state of emergency and revoke the increase in fuel prices. Mahuad explained that the agreement resulted from talks, and that he has given in on some points in order 'to stop the threat of confrontation between Ecuadorians, because the levels of violence might reach unimaginable heights'.

'I don't want to cause anybody problems. I was only seeking a way of out of the fiscal crisis the country is in.

Let us hope that by this agreement we can get on with one another again,' said the president.

Meanwhile, the armed forces issued a communiqué opposing any increase in the use of repressive force and rejecting 'any solution that would go against the democratic system'. The US ambassador to Ecuador, Leslie Alexander, told Mahuad that his government would not support a dictatorial solution, and pressed him to negotiate with the opposition to find a way out of the crisis. These statements suggest that Mahuad intended to carry out a government coup.

The government agreed to lower the price of fuel, but not to the level it was at before the adjustment measures. It also undertook to make the freezing of bank funds more flexible, and to withdraw all the privatisation bills for state enterprises. It accepted the opposition's tax proposals. VAT exemptions were abolished, except for on food and medicine. Taxes were imposed on banking utilities, luxury cars and capital gains.

'We have demonstrated indigenous power. We now have to wait and see if the government keeps its promise to impose taxes on banking utilities, luxury cars and capital gains. We have to wait and see whether it fulfils its promise to tax those who have most, as it agreed to do,' said Ricardo Ulcuango of CONAIE.

The largest cities have been paralysed by lack of public transport, road blocks set up by taxi drivers and barricades and demonstrations by citizens. In rural areas thousands of indigenous and peasants occupied roads and detained soldiers from the army, who were only set free in exchange for demonstrators who had been arrested previously. The peasants withheld their produce and there were shortages in city supermarkets. Lorries carrying animal and agricultural products towards the cites were stopped on the roads, and perishable foods began to rot. Milk products could not reach the pasteurisation plants, so milk became scarce in some cities.

People living in the crowded southern districts of Quito confronted the army, and set fire to an armoured vehicle. They prevented soldiers from dismantling the road blocks. Meanwhile, inhabitants of the surrounding districts of the port city of Guayaquil, the country's chief trading centre, resisted the intervention of the police and army and looted businesses.

In Cuenca, the country's third city, more than 30,000 people marched through the streets with placards demanding the repeal of the economic adjustment measures and the removal of Mahuad from the presidency.

In spite of the pact between the opposition and the government, the indigenous kept up their resistance 'as a way of guaranteeing that the agreements do not become a political deal that ignores the social sectors'.

The transport workers also decided to continue with their strike. They demanded that the price of petrol should be frozen and that the debts they contracted in dollars when they bought their vehicles should be converted into *sucres*. 'National mobilisation in the country and town forced the government to surrender. Possible agreements will only be accepted by the people if they reflect its will,' said the indigenous leader Miguel Lluco.

Former president, Rodrigo Borja, added to the uncertainty by stating that his opposition party, the Democratic Left (ID), had not reached any agreement with the government.

Borja demanded that petrol prices be reduced to their level before the measures imposed the previous week. Otherwise, he said, ID members of parliament would not vote for the proposed new taxes and there would be no majority in the house to see them through.

19 March 1999 (Friday) Thousands of indigenous people are keeping up their occupation of roads and villages throughout Ecuador in protest at the government's economic measures, despite the fact that president Jamil Mahuad has been meeting indigenous representatives to discuss their demands.

The mobilisation will continue until parliament satisfies the demands that caused the protests, particularly the unfreezing of bank deposits. So far the government and the single-chamber legislative parliament have agreed to the reduction in fuel prices, which brought to an end the strike by transport workers.

At dawn last Friday, indigenous groups took over a hydro-electric plant in the province of Tungurahua and cut off the electricity in various regions.

ANCESTRAL SORROWS, MODERN SORROWS

5 May 1999

JEREMY HORNER / PANOS PICTURES

The economic crisis has led to an increase in the number of cases of depression in Quito, Guayaquil and Cuenca, the country's principal cities, according to professional researchers. Growing unemployment, the freezing of bank accounts and the instability in the country has led to many Ecuadorians manifesting symptoms of depression.

Depression affects people of different ages and social classes and leads to increased numbers, especially of young people, attempting suicide. In the past six months 1,000 cases of attempted suicide have been registered.

Bernardo Arauz, a psychologist and member of the department of mental health at the Voz Andes Hospital, stated that 80 per cent of the reported suicides in this hospital over the past two years have been committed by adolescents.

Psychiatric doctor Luis Fierro says that the eco-nomic situation leads to families becoming unstable and failing to communicate, which becomes a breeding ground for depression. 'During the past few months many parents have been worried about coping with the crisis and have neglected their children. This lack of care and affection makes many young people think of suicide as an alternative,' he says.

In March inflation rose to 13.8 per cent, an historic figure, according to information from the National Institute of Statistics and Census. In the first quarter of the year, the accumulated increase in prices to the consumer reached 20.2 per cent and over the past 12 months the increase has been 54.3. per cent. 'People don't know how to cope with the crisis, and among the middle classes there have been cases of severe distress because of the freezing of bank accounts,' says Fierro.

According to the statistics, until last year the main cause of depression in cities was loneliness. In the first three months of this year, 70 per cent of cases are attributed directly or indirectly to the economic situation.

In the indigenous areas of the Ecuadorian Andes, as well as economic causes of depression there are cultural causes. In an Otavalo community, two hours north of Quito, in the province of Imbabura, Salvador spoke of his sadness and how it is difficult for him and so many of his companions to stop looking sad. He recalls a gentleman who travelled through that region investigating 'why he was sad', but he went away and never told him 'whether he had discovered the cause of his tears'. If – as some psychiatrists maintain – depression in cities can be the result of loneliness, with indigenous people of Quechua origin like Salvador, cultural causes, passed down from generation to generation, must also be taken into account.

Canadian doctor Michel Tousignant, who has lived in Ecuador for many years studying the Quechua people, was one of the first to note that depression also has cultural aspects. During his stay in the country he conducted an investigation on the *llaqui*, or sorrow, that affects Quechua and described it as an 'ideology of resignation, reflecting the psychology of being marginalised'. He stressed the importance of the cultural elements in this illness. To reach this conclusion he complemented his studies with the testimony of the indigenous themselves. They told him that from ancestral times many of them had suffered from this 'sadness disease' which had always been treated by shamans.

Despite the significance of this study, Tousignant was never able to pursue it further and most psychiatrists neither took much notice of it nor continued the investigation. That is why even today in Ecuador people still talk of llaqui as part of the mythology of the Quechua people.

But things began to change when Doctor Mario Maldonado (who had a master's degree in psychiatry from McGill University in Canada) decided to continue Tousignant's work, and put the investigation on a scientific basis. He proved that *llaqui* is what western medicine calls depression.

His work, entitled *Llaqui and Depression: An exploratory study among the Quechua of Ecuador*, was done in the city of Otavalo. There he investigated depression among different groups. Finally, he took 50 people suffering from the illness and made a psychiatric diagnosis. Maldonado had the help of 10 shamans or *yachactaitas*, who had used various treatments on their patients and developed certain theories about the illness.

Until recently Ecuadorian psychiatrists believed *llaqui* was merely a folk belief, with no clinical importance and therefore not needing medical treatment. As a result, whenever they were presented with a case of *llaqui* the doctors prescribed analgesics or vitamins, which eliminated the symptoms but did not cure the disease.

Before his research into 'Quechua sadness' in the rural area of Otavalo, Maldonado believed the same as his colleagues. But his investigation proved that people suffering from *llaqui* needed psychiatric treatment, because 'they have psychological disorders'. And according to a socio-economic study, '*llaqui* produces a very negative economic, psychological and social impact, not only on the person affected but on his family and even his community, because often the sufferer stops working and turns to drink. That is why it is necessary to find more effective ways of treating the disease.' In order to get this, the Ecuadorian doctor recommends that 'health workers who frequently come across cases of *llaqui* should not base their treatment solely on what is recommended by psychiatry, but should draw more on Quechua beliefs, which contribute a whole cultural way of dealing with the disease and how to treat it.' Thus western medicine and indigenous wisdom can combine to deal with the depression.

SORROW IN THE PIPELINE

6 May 1999

RHODRI JONES / PANOS PICTURES

The ancestral sorrow of the Quechuas is also reflected in the modern sadness of the communities that are not respected by the white-*mestizo* authorities. Indigenous communities in the province of Napo, in Ecuadorian Amazonia, are today protesting against the contamination of the River Misahuall', caused by the construction of an oil pipeline.[13]

Over the past two weeks villagers in this oil region have been alarmed by the increasing incidence of diarrhoea among children and the appearance of fungi on people's skin. Medical analysis established that these symptoms were caused by infections produced by drinking and using water from the river.

Indigenous leader Martha Tapuy says that the children are ill and lack medicines, which is why the communities are asking for 'the authorities to intervene'. 'The river is part of our lives. If we do not get water from it, there is nowhere else we can get it from,' she says.

The contamination is attributed to the waste thrown into the river by the company building the pipeline, which is not using adequate technology to protect the water, according to experts. Last week dozens of indigenous people occupied a bridge to prevent the company's workers from crossing it. They were confronted by soldiers and police before being moved off it.

In a neighbouring region, women and chil-

[13] Oil has dominated Ecuador's economic – and to a large extent political – life since large-scale production began in the 1970s. It was partly the desire to control this new-found source of wealth that prompted nationalists within the military to launch a coup in 1972, believing the oil should be exploited for the benefit of the nation rather than in the interests of the traditional political elite. The military government borrowed heavily against oil in order to industrialise Ecuador's economy, reduce imports and diversify exports. By the mid-1970s, the more radical officers had been replaced, and as debts mounted and

dren from the communities took over a retro-excavator belonging to the company and kidnapped the operators without harming them.

The indigenous people are demanding that the company stops building the pipeline and clean up the waters before continuing with its works. Until this happens, they are demanding rainwater tanks for daily drinking.

After the protests there were round-table talks between the governor of the province of Napo, Edgar Santillán, indigenous leaders of Ecuadorian Amazonia and executives of the oil company. The company undertook to comply with the communities' demands. However, the indigenous leaders said that they would keep on the alert and if the problem was not solved, they would take further actions, which could spread the conflict to Ecuador's other Amazon provinces.

Turquino Tapuy, leader of the Napo Federation of Indigenous Organisations, states that the damage done by the oil companies is not a new problem. He says: 'The communities do not have much confidence in the word of personnel belonging to these companies.'

The environmental organisation Ecological Action denounced the fact that 'the activity of oil companies in the East of Ecuador is destroying one of the world's most bio-diverse regions and seriously threatens the survival of many indigenous communities'.

Poor record

Problems caused by oil are not recent. In the 1930s the Shell Company conducted the first explorations of Amazonia. This introduced diseases, which cause the death of hundreds of indigenous Huaorani, who had no defences against them.

poverty rose again unrest grew, the generals were persuaded to hand power back at the end of the 1980s. Ecuador still does not have the refinery capacity to satisfy all of its domestic consumption. The oil sector has continued to dominate politics as successive governments have struggled to balance debt repayments. In 1987 Ecuador defaulted on its debt rescheduling after oil prices fell and an earthquake put the Trans-Ecuador Pipeline out of commission for months.

Oil was Ecuador's largest export at the beginning of the 1990s. Production increased from 78,000 barrels per day (bpd) in 1972 to 338,000 bpd in 1997. Export volume rose from 25 million barrels in 1992 to 91 million barrels in 1997. Although by 2000 oil and derivatives had fallen behind bananas in terms of export value, oil continues to be the biggest source

of income for the state. During the crisis of 1999-2000, the global oil boom gave Ecuador some breathing space as prices rose from US$8 per barrel in March 1999 to US$22 in September of the same year, passing US$24 in the first half of 2000.

Like Guayaquil, the Amazonian provinces have begun to demand autonomy and that income from oil should stay in the region, which is the one that suffers the worst environmental pollution as a result of oil extraction.

The Federation of Workers of Petroecuador (FETREPAC) is the most powerful union in the country after the National Union of Teachers (UNE). FETREPAC has the capacity to stop the pumping of oil and shipping of fuel, which are key to the Ecuadorian economy.

From 1967 to 1990 Texaco Petroleum Company had a monopoly on oil exploitation in Amazonia. Later the state enterprise Petroecuador and 10 foreign companies took over. When Texaco withdrew, indigenous peoples, supported by environmental organisations, pursued a claim against the company in the United States for the damage and environmental destruction wrought during the years it had been exploiting oil in the area. The protestors demonstrated that the company had not been using environmental protection technology in common use in other places where oil was extracted. This caused contamination of rivers and irreparable damage to the flora and fauna of the region.

Recent Ecuadorian governments, including that of Jamil Mahuad, did not support the legal action against Texaco, and asked the US courts to transfer jurisdiction in the case to Ecuador, which was supported by the oil company. But the case is continuing in the United States and it is hoped that in the next few months the US court will force the company to decontaminate the

affected areas and indemnify the indigenous communities.

Valerio Grefo, indigenous member of parliament for Amazonia, points out that it is vital to help communities affected by oil contamination to avoid a health disaster. 'Apart from the fact that irreversible health problems might occur, this is an attack on our people's symbols, their world and when that happens all they can do is fight,' says Grefo.

Dolphins in danger

Recently there was more alarming news about Ecuadorian Amazonia. The pink dolphin, one of the rarest species in the region, is in danger of extinction. Biologist Judith Denkinger, a pink dolphin specialist, warned that these animals might disappear if there is no halt to deforestation and the contamination of the waters of the Rivers Cuyabeno, Aguarico, Lagarto and other rivers they inhabit.

In 1993 an oil spill in Shushfindi contaminated the River Aguarico and caused the death of many dolphins. In the past six years other oil spills and deforestation have pushed other cetaceous creatures to the point of extinction.

The dolphins that managed to survive took refuge in more inaccessible rivers and lakes on the frontier between Peru and Ecuador, where Denkinger set up an observatory to study their behaviour. With the signing of peace between the two countries, further exploitation of the region was announced, extending the threat of oil contamination to the last havens of the pink dolphin. Denkinger says that if deforestation and oil contamination of the rivers is not stopped, this species, unique in the world, will disappear.

'All that will remain', says Denkinger, 'will be the indigenous legend, according to which the pink dolphins each turn into a man or a woman to seek their mate in the riverside communities and that when they find him or her, they return to the river together and turn back into dolphins.'

◀ Pictures left, far left and on page 25 show children playing near where wastes from oil production in Shushfindi, north-eastern Ecuador, are being burnt off.

RECLAIMING THE LAND

10 May 1999

Forced to live high in the mountain, on the dry barren plateau, without health services, without work, without much land, the peasants of Licto, a small corner of Chimborazo, were obliged to exploit every tiny bit of land. 'Over time the land became weak and there was almost nowhere left to plant. Some went off to the city in order to survive. The rest of us remained here, fighting to get the lower lands which had belonged to our ancestors, and doing the best we could to make the high lands produce a little,' says an indigenous inhabitant of the region.

Joining forces, the local indigenous people began working to recover the lands which had been abandoned. 'For us, recovering the land is like recovering our culture, recovering our life and the life of our grandparents. We are getting along fine,' says Emilio a leader of the Indigenous Movement of Chimborazo (MICH) , a branch of CONAIE.

By traditional indigenous methods, which they had stopped using decades ago, lands which had become desert began to produce. The hard Ecuadorian clay (*cangahua*) began to become fertile land.

They used terraces, low stone walls and trenches and native trees for protection. Thus agro-forestation has helped the peasants of Licto in their struggle for a little plot of land to cultivate. 'We have recovered lands which were unproductive in the hands of the big landowners, thanks to our struggle. But as well as this we are recovering ground which no one ever imagined could one day be cultivated. Many say we are mad but time has proved us right. Thus we are demonstrating that it is possible to produce collectively and we are doing it,' says Emilio.

As well as using traditional Andean techniques to protect their crops, they have also begun re-foresting the mountain, which over the past 50 years had lost all its forest. Native trees were important in the protection of crops, because

SEAN SPRAGUE / PANOS PICTURES

they prevented erosion and protected the crops from hard rain. They set up two nurseries of native trees, which supply the necessary young trees to re-forest the area.

Minga (communal labour) and mutual help enabled the various communities of Licto to remain united. '*Minga* is a way of working in solidarity, which is rooted in our culture. It is a way we Indians have of helping each other and helping the community. The work of recovering land is done in *mingas* and our people all share in it. Then what is produced on this land is for everybody,' says Josefa, an indigenous woman of the region.

In the past few years another wish of the communities of Licto and Chimborazo has been fulfilled. This is the implementation of an irrigation system which has helped improve production. Nevertheless, as yet there is not much water for the peasants of Chimborazo and other regions in the Sierra, and the high plateau land is cracking.

The indigenous people are convinced that land recovery is just part of seeing the world in a different way and building a better life.

THE ECONOMY ISN'T WORKING
18 June 1999

The latest report on the Ecuador labour market produced by the firm Cedatos has revealed that only 27.5 per cent of the economically active population is in full time work, contradicting the electoral promises of president Jamil Mahuad.

From the time Mahuad took over the presidency in August 1998 until the end of May 1999, unemployment rose from 13 to 18.1 per cent and under-employment was 54.4 per cent.

Polivio Córdoba, director of Cedatos, said Mahuad's promise to create 900,000 jobs 'not only was not fulfilled but the situation actually got worse'. Córdoba recalled that 'this promise to create jobs was one of the main reasons for his victory'.[14]

Of an economically active population of 3.5. million people, '72.5 per cent were unemployed or employed part time. The main worry of those in work is that they might lose their job,' said Córdoba.

Between August 1998 and May 1999, 141,000 people were unemployed, and during this period 22,000 Ecuadorians who found jobs did not find the kind of work they wanted. Many of those counted as in work were on temporary contracts, and the majority of firms had decided to apply job-flexibility and to eliminate most fixed contracts so as to avoid having to pay the taxes due for a worker on a long-term contract.

Jorge Vivanco Mendieta, political analyst and sub-director of the leading daily *Expreso*, said the economic crisis and its effect on employment had been caused by the politico-economic policy pursued over the past 20 years, including by the

present government. 'The principal people directing the country's economic policy for the last 20 years have remained the same,' Vivanco said.

He said: 'The policy of the state financial organisations has been managed by a small group of people, representing the interests of power groups whose greed produced an unjust distribution of wealth, and who used fiscal policy for their own benefit.'

Alberto Acosta, an economic analyst, said the Ecuadorian scene presents a depressing picture with an unpromising outlook. In 1998 the trade deficit exceeded US$1 billion, reversing the positive trend that had existed since 1979; international monetary reserves fell from US$1.8 billion in August 1998 to US$1.3 billion in May 1999.

March 1999 showed the highest monthly inflation for many years, at 13.5 per cent. In 1998 the fiscal deficit reached US$1.2 billion, or 6 per cent of gross national product (GNP). It looks as if it may rise to 7.3 per cent for 1999. In 1999 a 6 per cent fall in GNP is expected, which would add to the recessive trend.

In 1999 the US dollar rose from 7,500 *sucres* in January to its present (June 1999) rate of 10,300 *sucres*, peaking in March at nearly 19,000 *sucres*. 'The devaluation is equivalent to 90 per cent. This situation affects economic agents with debts in dollars, which constitute 60 per cent of credits. These firms see laying off staff as a way of reducing costs,' said Alberto Acosta.

He believes the crisis has been partly caused by the effects of the climatic phenomenon El Niño, which according to the Permanent Commission for Latin America (CEPAL), led to the loss of US$2.9 billion dollars and expenditure of more than US$700 million. It also caused a fall in oil prices and exports. 'The import of Asian products triggers immediate unemployment because national industry in competition with them loses

[14] Jamil Mahuad was elected president in July 1998, as a candidate for the centrist Democrácia Popular (DP – Popular Democracy). As mayor of Quito for two terms he had built a popular support base, which he consolidated by signing the peace agreement with Peru in October 1998.

its sales and therefore reduces its workforce,' he said.

Another burden is servicing the foreign debt, which eats up nearly half the state budget, while health workers, administrators, university and school teachers and other public sector workers have not been paid for two months. Teachers were paid their April salary with cheques that bounced. 'Servicing the Brady bonds (commercial debt) in the early weeks of 1999 left the treasury coffers empty and forced the government to suspend the payment of salaries to public sector workers for the first quarter of the year,' the economist said.[15]

Acosta believes that Mahuad's government had handled the crisis badly. 'He preferred to

meet the demands of financial capital and thus permitted the crisis, that was in the making when he took over the government, to grow. It has now reached extremely worrying heights,' he said.

Acosta considers it was destabilising to approve an unfunded budget for 1999, to eliminate income tax and to put a tax on the circulation of capital which takes 1 per cent of every financial transaction. Acosta says this new tax increased speculative pressure, because many economic agents opted to buy dollars and take them out of the country in order to avoid paying it. 'And it was a disincentive to providers of financial services, because many medium and small savers chose not to use banks any more, which had a negative impact on the weakened banking system,' he said.

According to Acosta, these measures were complemented by the desire to speed up the privatisation of oil electricity, telephones and ports. 'In his eagerness to reduce the size of the state and the number of functionaries running it, Mahuad eliminated public sector bodies and privatised others, which were not necessarily in deficit. This led to unemployment,' he says.

He also claims that the one-year freeze on bank deposits was closely connected to the fall in employment, because it caused businesses to close. On 11 March the government froze for one year half the balances of current accounts and

[15] Ecuador's foreign debt, at US$16 billion in May 2000, is the highest in Latin America in terms of gross domestic product – representing 84 per cent of GDP. Just over half (52 per cent) is owed to private banks, 30 per cent to multilateral creditors and the remaining 18 per cent to the Paris Club members. Ecuador earmarks 54 per cent of the national budget for debt repayment. In 1999 it paid out US$2.4 billion in interest on the debt, but declared a moratorium on the payment of Brady Bonds, which account for some US$6 billion of the country's debt. Brady Bonds take their name from the US treasury secretary Nicholas Brady who organised the financing plan to overcome the Latin America debt crisis which broke in 1982. The plan involved the reduction of the principal, and the refinancing of payment on the remaining capital owed and on interest accrued. Old debts were replaced by bonds backed by a deposit on the US Federal Reserve and the endorsement of the US

treasury. When Ecuador signed up to the Brady plan in 1994, foreign banks wrote down 30 per cent of the balance owing in return for a guarantee that the capital would be paid. In June 1999 the Group of Seven (G7) industrialised countries cancelled US$70 billion of debt of the world's poorest and most indebted countries – among them Bolivia, El Salvador, Honduras and Nicaragua. Ecuador was excluded on the basis of income per capita. In December 1998 the archbishop of Cuenca, Luis Alberto Luna Tobar proposed a joint negotiation among the Andean countries. 'There needs to be an international agreement with countries in the same desperate state Ecuador not to pay the external debt, or at least to reduce the damage done by these payments,' said the archbishop. 'There is a need for the the powerful to give a little and show some concern for those who have less.'

savings account over US$200 and all the deposits in current and term accounts in foreign currency over US$500. The freeze affected US$2.5 billion belonging to the 3.5 million Ecuadorians with bank accounts. 'The freeze was intended as a way of saving the financial system, by transferring working capital and savings belonging to individuals to the bank, because the state did not have resources to get through the crisis,' Acosta said.

According to the labour ministry, between January and April 1999 more than 400 small and medium-sized companies went bankrupt, leading to more than 90,000 job losses. Business sources said that in April 100 small and medium-sized firms closed, leaving 30,000 people unemployed. Meanwhile, some large firms such as Jaboner'a Nacional, Sumesa y Grasas Unico first laid off staff and then stopped production, giving their employees leave.[16]

Vivanco of El Expreso does not see an easy solution, because he believes that 'economic and political policy continues to be dominated by the same power groups. They will stay until a leader appears who is capable of breaking through this political and civic inertia, which is the basis of the crisis overwhelming us,' he said.

[16] Ecuador's industrial sector empoys 20 per cent of the workforce, while 45 per cent are in services and 35 per cent in agriculture. More than 200 industrial companies failed in 1999, putting 45,000 people out of work. Some large companies in Guayaquil, such as Jabonería Nacional (a producer of cleaning products), and Sumesa y Grasas Unico (foodstuffs), affected by the economic crisis in 1999 decided to reduce their workforce and gave early holidays to employees in months when there was no production. By May 2000 these companies were producing again but not at the same rate as in 1998. Principal exports are bananas, oil, and shrimp (see Table 1, page 14).

OIL AND CANCER
1 July 1999

A medical report reveals a high incidence of cancer among indigenous communities inhabiting oil-producing areas in Ecuador. The research was carried out in the oil zone of the north-eastern provinces of Sucumb'os and Orellana, in the Amazon region on the frontier with Colombia.

The results indicate that the people of the region have three times the risk of contracting cancer faced by people in other parts of the country.

The situation is worse with particular forms of cancer. For example, the risk of cancer of the larynx is 30 times greater than in other parts of the country. The risk of cancer of the gallbladder is 18 times greater, the risk of liver or skin cancer is 15 times greater and of stomach cancer five times greater.

The research was carried out by a medical team from the Department of Social Pastoral Work of the Vicariate of Aguarico, with the collaboration of experts from the organisation Medicus Mundi and the University of London Institute of Hygiene and Tropical Medicine.

The study, which took six months, was based on analysis of the water of the rivers, the study of affected populations and the statistical investigation of the growth of the incidence of cancer in relation to the increased oil production over the past 30 years. The incidence of cancer in this region was also compared with that in other non-oil regions of the country. A direct link was established between the appearance of the illness and oil contamination.

Miguel San Sebastián from Medicus Mundi

warns of the risk to health of continuing oil pro-duction without environmental control. 'The rivers are habitually used by the inhabitants of the area. They are contaminated with oil in a propor-tion 200 and 300 times greater than the limit per-mitted in human drinking water,' says San Sebastián.

This is the first medical report to establish a real relationship between the appearance of can-cer in a region where it did not exist before and contamination by oil mining. 'It is a warning to the authorities. It brings proof that while sources of contamination persist, the health of this and other similar populations will continue to be seri-ously affected,' said San Sebastián.

In January the government prohibited the extraction of crude oil in 135,000 hectares of humid tropical woodland belonging to the reserves of Cuyabeno and Yasun', situated in the north east. These areas, declared biosphere reserves by the United Nations Education, Science and Culture Organisation (UNESCO), are considered fragile because as well as their bio-

diversity, the very survival of the Quechua, Siona and Cofán communities in Cuyabeno and of the Huaorani in Yasun' is threatened.

Turquino Tapuy, an indigenous leader in Amazonia, doubts whether the decree will be have an effect: 'All governments make promises of this kind and then the exploitation goes on.'

The environmental organisation Ecological Action has denounced the fact that 'Oil activity in the east of Ecuador is destroying one of the regions of greatest biodiversity on the whole planet. It also threatens the survival of many indigenous communities.'

Amoco-Mobil, Arco, City, CGC, Elf, Oryx, Pérez Companc, Santa Fe, Tripetrol and Triton are foreign companies operating in the Amazon region, extracting oil from areas which have been officially declared natural reserves.

Despite the fact that oil from the Amazon region has contributed greatly to the state finances, only 3 per cent of the national budget is reinvested in the region, which has the highest poverty levels in the country.

BLOOD SELLS
2 July 1999

At least 10 samples of Ecuadorian indigenous blood are to be found on sale in so-called 'Genome Boutiques' in the United States. This international biological trade offers blood sam-ples for scientific investigation in the area of bio-genetics. In this way, the genes of the indigenous Tsáchila, Chachis, Huaoranis and Amazonian Quechuas crossed the frontiers of Ecuador. Yet these peoples never gave consent for experi-ments with their blood.

The Medical Investigations Institute Coriell Cell Repositories has a vast collection in which samples are to be found from different indige-nous peoples of Latin America. Scientists at the

institute check the DNA and then sell each sam-ple for US$100 to laboratories and universities. They even sell it on the internet.

The samples that have already been sold form part of the investigation of the human genome, which is taking place in the United States and Europe. As an example of these studies evidence can be shown that in the investigation of the tis-sue of the Chachis a genetic characteristic of immunity was discovered, known as HLA, which is exclusive to this people. The discovery, which may be of the greatest importance in increasing immunity against AIDS, is cited in the text *The Genetic Characterisation of the Cayapa Indians and its Relationship with other American Populations.* The study was directed by the Department of Biology of the University of Rome. How did these samples reach these institutions or the genome boutiques? There is very little information about this and the Ecuadorian scientific community says that it was not even aware of this type of international study.

The little information we have suggests the samples were taken by members of certain Pentecostal sects, expelled some years ago from the country.

As well as the samples from indigenous Ecuadorians, there are indigenous samples from Venezuela, Colombia, Panama and Brazil.

Indigenous representatives from Colombia and Ecuador have decided to initiate a joint international legal action to recover the samples. They are hoping for the support of ecological and human rights organisations from other countries. In addition they are pushing within their own countries for a law to protect biodiversity. Various groups of ecologists, the Canadian Centre for Investigation into Biopiracy and the International Foundation for the Development of Rural Populations have called for 'opposition to such programmes which show the racist character of science in the First World, because many of the experiments are directed towards a supposed improvement of the human race'.

The indigenous leader Ricardo Ulcuango says: 'This is not only an attack on the biological diversity of our country but also on the human rights of indigenous peoples. It is an outrage committed by the powerful nations against our peoples.'

There are countless examples of exploitation of the biological resources of Ecuador without any benefit to the country, also called bio-piracy. Nevertheless, 'Never before have they reached the point of carrying off our brothers' and sisters' blood,' says Ulcuango.

The Declaration on the Human Genome, adopted by United Nations Organisation for Education, Science and Culture (UNESCO), lays down ethical guidelines for genetic investigation. This declaration says: 'Before there is any investi-

gation of this kind, there must be a full study of its potential risks and benefits.' It indicates that any sample must be taken with the consent of the person, who has the right to decide whether he or she wishes to be informed of the results of the study.

The same declaration says the genetic material of each individual is the common heritage of humanity, and therefore must not produce economic profit. Countries of the Andean Pact[17] must abide by resolution 391 of the Carthage Agreement, which demands bilateral contracts between governments and companies interested in access to genetic resources. But it makes clear that in the indigenous case, the first to be consulted must be the communities.

The Convention on Biodiversity, which has the force of international law, says that biological resources come within the area of national sovereignty. It also states the need for consent and participation by those who possess the resources, who should benefit from sharing them. Knowledge, participation and access require that both the state and the indigenous peoples should know the true goal of the research and should benefit from it.

Santiago Carrasco, president of the Ecuador Foundation for Science and Technology (FUNDACYT), believes there is 'an inviolable principle which must be respected in genetic investigation: that of human dignity'. Carrasco, who considers this principle has been violated, says it is 'fundamentally important that there should be legislation to protect the biodiversity of Ecuador'.

[17] Bolivia, Colombia, Ecuador, Peru and Venezuela.

MAURICIO USHIÑA

The huípala returns to the streets

6 July 1999 (Tuesday) The indigenous people of Ecuador are keeping up their occupation of roads in protest against the decision by Jamil Mahuad's government to raise the price of fuel and insist on the privatisation of public organisations.

Thousands of people came out of their communities to block roads and prevent agricultural goods getting to market.

The protest called by CONAIE will go on until the government shelves its privatisation law. Antonio Vargas, president of CONAIE, says the government does not care about the opinions of Ecuador's indigenous peoples. With the raising of fuel prices and the onslaught of privatisations, they have no option but to protest. 'The indigenous nations and the social movements continue to be open to dialogue, but Mahuad's government does not want to listen. We do not want to give away our patrimony, as they did in Argentina and Chile, and then have to suffer power cuts,' said Vargas.

Last week parliament considered a bill introduced by the executive, which grants special powers to Mahuad to decide on the sale of state enterprises. The opposition came out against the bill, but the government announced that in two weeks' time it will introduce another, after seeking agreements with sectors that accept privatisation but disagree with special powers.

Yesterday 45,000 taxi drivers came out on strike against the increase in fuel prices decreed on Friday by the finance minister Ana Lucía Armijos. They demanded her resignation. The strike paralysed 60 per cent of the country, and the streets of the main cities were cut off. In some provinces the indigenous communities joined the taxi drivers and blocked the principal roads. Classes were suspended in all educational establishments.

A state of emergency had been in force since Monday. The armed forces were mobilised and the right to assemble or hold meetings was suspended. On Monday night members of the police Special Operations Group invaded the premises of the taxi drivers' union and arrested those they found there. Union leaders who were not arrested went underground, and the security forces arrested more than 80 demonstrators.

Government minister Vladimiro Alvarez Grau said he would not accept the strikers' conditions because president Mahuad was the one to govern Ecuador. He stressed the president's authority, which has been questioned by analysts and members of the government itself, who have claimed that the government was being run by the finance minister. Alvarez said the government was 'open to dialogue', but would not agree to discuss the resignation of Armijos.

Rumours of a coup were confirmed by Monsignor José Eguiguren, secretary of the Ecuadorian Bishops' Conference (CEE), who said no one should consider dictatorship as a solution. Eguiguren said on Radio La Luna de Quito that the country was going through dramatic times and that it was necessary to create spaces for transparent dialogue, taking into account the deep economic crisis and the hardship suffered by the middle classes and the poor.

He also said solutions must be sought beyond the pressures of certain powerful groups, who only wanted to benefit themselves. He stressed that a non-democratic way out would make the country's situation even worse. 'The government must make the

gesture of revising its measures. It is vital that it shows sensitivity to the poorest. It is alarming to see that teachers and doctors are not being paid their wages of 1.5 million *sucres* (US$150 dollars),' said Eguiguren.

Rumours of a coup were fueled by the presence in the country of Charles Wilhelm, chief of the southern command of the US army, who met representatives of the government behind closed doors.

Ecuador is facing its worst economic crisis for 30 years, with unemployment at 18.1 per cent, and under-employment at 54.4. per cent. This year the government has to pay out US$2.4 billion to service the foreign debt. The failure of 10 banks in the past eight months has already cost the state US$1.6 billion dollars.

Miguel Lluco of the opposition Pachakutik Movement said, 'The national mobilisation in the country and town made the government back down in March and it will again now. We believed it would not be necessary to have another uprising but the government is pushing us into it. Let us hope the Bishops' Conference will be able to mediate and talk some sense into Mahuad, otherwise we will remain on strike indefinitely,' said Lluco.

9 July 1999 (Friday) The national protest against the Ecuadorian government intensified today, when more than 3,000 indigenous from the province of Tungurahua in the central Sierra, occupied radio and television stations and cut off their signals.

The president of CONAIE, Antonio Vargas, said that if the government does not put things right, by Monday there would be an all-out uprising. Vargas made public a document by the International Monetary Fund (IMF), which recommends that the government increase the price of gas by 105 per cent. He said that if the military repressed the protest, there would be confrontations.

The indigenous and peasants announced that they proposed to take over hydroelectric and drinking water treatment plants, and to block the transit of essential products. The first measure was the closure of roads, which prevented livestock fairs and agricultural markets from being held. It also prevented farm products from being transported from the communities to the cities. As supplies have begun to run short in Quito and Guayaquil prices of the few fruits and vegetables to be found in the supermarkets have risen by 60 and 120 per cent since last week. The gas shortage is beginning to be felt and petrol may soon run short.

There is no public transport in Quito, Guayaquil, Cuenca and other cities. Buses are not running because the taxi drivers' strike has closed off streets.

According to the National Directorate of Police Operations, there have been 273 arrests since the beginning of the protest.

Government minister Vladimiro Alvarez Grau offered transport workers a preferential price on fuel in exchange for ending their protest. However, in the absence of Pedro Alava, the main leader of the National Federation of Taxi Drivers, they were unable to reach an agreement. The organisation confirmed that it is not going to take part in the talks until the state of emergency is lifted and arrested taxi drivers are set free. From his hiding place, Alava stated that the transport unions negotiating with the government for the lifting of the strike are not representative.

At the invitation of the government and CONAIE, the Ecuadorian bishops'

conference agreed to mediate in the conflict. Vargas stated that CONAIE would join in the talks, provided the most recent fuel price rise is cancelled, the state of emergency is lifted and those arrested on the protests are set free.

Parliament could not meet to discuss the lifting of the state of emergency for lack of a quorum.

Some 76 per cent of the population support the taxi drivers' strike and the indigenous uprising, according to a poll by the firm Cedatos carried out this week in Quito and Guayaquil. However, most people consulted said they were not taking part in the strike 'for fear of losing their job' or because going out on the streets to protest 'would affect the family budget'.

The protests led to an IMF mission, which was supposed to arrive in Ecuador this Thursday, being postponed until 'the internal political atmosphere returns to normal'. This meant the postponement of the signing of a letter of intent with the IMF, which Mahuad was expecting to sign on 16 July.

10 July 1999 (Saturday) CONAIE affirmed that the uprising will be intensified this coming Monday with acts of civil disobedience in the cities. The indigenous have a three-point platform: cancellation of the increase in fuel prices, freezing of petrol and gas prices and the release of taxi drivers arrested this week.

Since Friday, 8,000 indigenous in the province of Tungurahua in the central Sierra, 100 km from Quito, have taken over radio and television stations and cut their signal. The indigenous went up the mountain, more than 4,200 metres above sea level, and without giving the 12 caretakers time to react, they stationed themselves nearby. A contingent of 80 army soldiers tried to remove them, but the demonstrators blocked access routes to the antennae with trees, rocks and trenches. The soldiers then flew over the area by helicopter.

Vicente Chato, leader of CONAIE in the area, said that the sight of the helicopter enraged the indigenous, who raised their machetes and cut the booster cables, so that some television channels and radio stations could not broadcast.

About 100 metres from the place where they found the indigenous, armed soldiers began descending from the helicopter. They were surrounded by peasants, who told them that if they intended to take action there would be a confrontation. In the same helicopter the provincial governor and media bosses came to negotiate.

The indigenous leaders agreed to restore the signal but said they would not leave until the government had lifted its measures. They announced that they were preparing a march on Quito by thousands of indigenous people. The protest by taxi drivers and indigenous has been joined by members of Seguro Campesino[18], teachers, oil workers, health workers, and street traders mobilising in various cities.

[18] Seguro Social Campesino is a state fund that provides medical assistance and pensions for 3 million peasants, and is closely linked to the indigenous movement. Threatened privatisation could lead to the removal of peasants' medical cover and pensions. Organisations affiliated to Seguro Campesino, representing small producers and other peasant sectors, together have the greatest capacity for mobilisation in Ecuador next to the indigenous organisations.

PAINTING THE WORLD
11 July 1999

Dozens of members of the five communities forming part of the Tigua canton, in the province of Cotopaxi, are preparing to march on Latacunga, the provincial capital, where they will meet with thousands more to take over the city, as part of the indigenous uprising which is paralysing the country.

The majority of the 3,500 indigenous from the region make a living by painting, which the whole family takes part.

In the central region of the Ecuadorian mountain range, particularly in Chimborazo, Cotopaxi and Tungurahua, for many years the indigenous people decorated the heads of their great drums with festive paintings. In this way the mountain, animals, plants, ponchos, hats and harvest became part of the drums which embodied an ancestral culture.

But they needed to spread their art beyond their region and so they began to paint this whole world on leather – today dried, stretched sheep skins are used – which were then taken to other parts of the country. Throughout the region of Tigua women, children, men and old people spend most of their time doing this work.

The region's landscapes, the fairs, festivals, the old life on the great estates, the Mass, home life, the work of painters themselves as they create their pictures, the struggle for land, the struggle of the indigenous movement and many other images are stamped on the leather.

In the homes of the inhabitants of Tigua we found pictures in all sizes, which would later be taken to Quito and other cities to be sold in the craft shops, where they generally get good prices from tourists. 'It's a good income for us,' says

'El Shaman' by Julio Toaquiza of Tigua-Chimbacucho.

Pedro, an indigenous artists from Tigua. 'Even though the craft shop takes much more than we sell them for, it is our best way of selling them. Of course, if we could sell directly to the public, it would be better, but that is difficult because we do not have premises in the areas where tourists go.'

Although Tigua painting is a tradition rooted in these communities of the Ecuadorian mountains, the art had become debased because the emphasis was only on the commercial. 'The problem,' says Pedro, 'is that many mestizo artists from the city started producing work similar to Tigua paintings because it was good business. But the way they looked at things was not indigenous, it had nothing to do with our communities. It ceased to be indigenous art, and sales dropped a lot.'

There are not many people painting today; they have to march to Latacunga.

12 July 1999 (Monday) The government of Ecuador is cornered by protests that are paralysing the country, in a climate of social upheaval similar to that immediately before the fall of president Abdalá Bucaram in February 1997.

Yesterday 10,000 indigenous people took the city of Latacunga, capital of the central province of Cotopaxi, 70 km south of Quito. They cut off the entry bridge to the city in protest against the increase in fuel prices decreed last week, and against the privatisation bill.

Hours later 100 soldiers of the army arrived and tried to disperse the indigenous protestors with tear gas, but they only succeeded in enraging them. The military opened fire on the crowd and wounded 12 people. Several were shot in the back, one of whom was Segundo Bedoya, who got a bullet in his backbone and is in danger of dying or being paralysed.

The action provoked fierce street protests from the city's inhabitants, joined by many indigenous who had come in from the surrounding areas. The soldiers fled in lorries and although they had been identified as belonging to a local barracks, the authorities claimed they were not from the area and that they did not know where they had come from.

CONAIE leaders announced that they would sue the government for attempted murder and step up their protests. Indigenous leader Ricardo Ulcuango, blamed the defence minister, retired general José Gallardo, for the military attack on the indigenous protestors. 'The military repression was against a peaceful demonstration and our brothers and sisters were shot in the back, as medical evidence shows. The defence minister must explain this,' said Ulcuango. He said he would not accept excuses or 'lies that they know how to invent in situations like this'. 'We want justice,' he said.

As well as Latacunga, other towns in the province were taken over to prevent markets from being held and products reaching them. In the province of Tungurahua, bordering Cotopaxi, the situation is similar. Since Friday the radio and television stations have been occupied and broadcasting interrupted.

This morning about a thousand indigenous and peasant women from the northern province of Imbabura, led by Blanca Chancoso[19], began a 200 km march on the capital. They plan to link with other women starting out from different provinces to enter the capital together. 'We are indigenous women fighting for better days,' says Chancoso.

'Our brothers and sisters are marching peacefully, so we hope that there will be no repression and that they will not be arrested, because they are ready to respond,' said Antonio Vargas, president of CONAIE.

Seeing the siege closing in on the government, president Jamil Mahuad announced a freeze on current fuel prices until 31 December. Mahuad explained that the price of a barrel of oil had increased above US$15, and this enabled him to keep down the price of fuel without increasing his fiscal deficit.

Miguel Lluco asked whether the authorities were unaware that the price of a barrel of oil had risen to US$15 the week before. 'This government is again showing its negligence. Why did it wait till now to announce the price freeze? Did it want us to reach this situation?' he asked.

Spokespersons for different social organisations say that the measure announced by Mahuad does not go far enough. They are demanding that fuel

[19] CONAIE's secretary for international relations.

LORI WASELCHUK

A meeting in Imbabura

prices should be frozen at the level they were at before the last increase.

Some sectors are demanding the president's resignation, but Lluco did not think this would be a solution because if Mahuad resigned, his place would be taken by the vice-president or the president of parliament, whom he considers to be even worse. 'This situation must be put right. Let them change their economic policy, remove the minister of finance, show concern for the lives of the poor and stop giving money to corrupt bankers. If they don't, the country will catch fire and no one will be able to control it,' he said.

All the provincial capitals are paralysed, without buses or taxis. Shortages are beginning to bite, with a lack of food supplies and of gas. Petrol is also expected to become scarce soon. Since 5 July there has been a state of

emergency throughout the country, with suspension of the rights to assemble and hold meetings. The armed forces have been mobilised. According to the National Directorate of Police Operations, 320 people have been arrested since the protests began.

16 July 1999 (Friday) The conflict between transport workers and the government which paralysed Ecuador for 12 days ended today. But 15,000 indigenous have announced that they will remain in the capital until their demands are met.

The indigenous people who have marched peacefully into Quito since yesterday, were severely repressed by the army. The army has blocked the streets of Quito and surrounded the government palace, where president Jamil Mahuad is negotiating with the different sectors in conflict. A number of indigenous protesters received bullet wounds during the march into the capital.

At the southern entrance to the city, marchers were welcomed by the inhabitants. But more than 1,500 military arrived in lorries and helicopters, throwing tear gas into the crowd and firing shots in the air. With all the main access streets to the capital guarded by army personnel, the indigenous devised ways of getting in by country roads.

On Wednesday Mahuad said he was prepared to review the rise in fuel prices and to create a development fund for the indigenous nations, but he did not say how he would do this. Indigenous leader Ricardo Ulcuango said Mahuad's words had opened a door to dialogue. However, the military attack on the indigenous people seems to close it again. 'The president is used to lying to us. That is why, until his promises are put into practice, we do not believe them. He has not lifted the state of emergency, which is a basis for any talks,' said Ulcuango.

The Ecuadorian single-chamber parliament has approved an amnesty for more than 500 prisoners, proposed by Gilberto Talahua, a member of parliament for Pachakutik. But it is thought that the releases will take a long time. 'The state of siege continues. Social leaders are in prison and the army violently repressed our brothers and sisters who came in from all corners of the country on a peaceful march,' Talahua told the press agency Inter Press Service.

Ulcuango said the indigenous movement would continue its uprising and the peasants who had entered Quito would not leave the city until the prisoners were released.

Three people have died – including one 14-year-old girl – and there has been an unknown number of arrests since the strike began. Army attacks on the indigenous in different parts of the Sierra left dozens with bullet wounds. Some people are in a critical condition and might be permanently paralysed. There were cases of suffocation throughout the country and a little girl hit by a tear gas bomb was blinded. At least 300 of the more than 500 arrested during the strike were to be brought before the military courts. Among these were 56 leaders of the demonstrations. The rest were taxi drivers, citizens obstructing roads and a few workers.

Human rights organisations say the government's behaviour during these protests confirms Ecuador as being among countries with the worst human rights violations. Amnesty International has denounced the death squad in Guayaquil, the torture and murder of the socialist trade unionist Saúl Cañar, and the murder of the left-wing member of parliament

---

'This government is committing grave human rights violations by declaring this state of emergency to check social discontent, which has its origin in the hard economic measures affecting the majority of the population,'
– Elsie Monge, director of the Ecumenical Commission for Human Rights

Jaime Hurtado, in which a police collaborator was implicated.[20]

Amnesty also mentioned the death of two people in the province of Manabí at the hands of para-police and police, the arrest and torture of a columnist on the daily paper *El Universo* and the systematic forced entry into the homes of people in Guayaquil who have no known criminal connection.

Elsie Monge, director of the Ecumenical Commission for Human Rights (CEDHU), said that she was concerned about the repression of the indigenous and various social movements protesting against the government. 'This government is committing grave human rights violations by declaring this state of emergency to check social discontent, which has its origin in the hard economic measures affecting the majority of the population,' said Monge, a Catholic nun. She added

that the declaration of the state of emergency violated the American Convention and the United Nations Pact on Civil and Political Rights. Monge said the application of the national security law to try civilians by the military code violated the right to be judged by independent and impartial courts. 'On the one hand the armed forces are active agents during the state of emergency, and on the other, the army courts are sitting in judgment on non-military matters, which affect civilians,' she said.

According to a poll published today by the firm Cedatos, 87 per cent of Ecuadorians do not trust the word of president Mahuad and 86 per cent disapprove of his way of running the country. His popularity, which stood at 66 per cent a year ago, has dropped to 11 per cent.

[20] **Human rights in Ecuador** The worst period for human rights in Ecuador's recent history was during the government of León Febres Cordero (1984-88), when there was severe repression of popular sectors, assassinations and disappearance of people linked to the left and social movements. The repression also included young people with no active political or social links – as in the case of the Restrepo brothers, two minors abducted by police in January 1988. Although the state admitted responsibility they are still among the disappeared and the case has not been resolved. The same happened with the majority of cases in this period, and impunity persists despite the hard work of the Ecumenical Commission on Human Rights.

During the government of Jamil Mahuad the leader of the Movimiento Popular Democrático (MPD) Jaime Hurtado was assassinated. He was shot in broad daylight in February 1999, just 30 metres from the supreme court building. Different sources claim 'para-police' were involved and people linked to the Mahuad government, but the crime goes unpunished. The killer of the trades unionist Saul Canar – whose body was

found in late 1998 showing signs of torture – also enjoys impunity. During the indigenous uprising of July 1999 the armed forces and police attacked indigenous in various parts of the Sierra, leaving one dead, dozens with bullet wounds, and others injured by tear-gas. There has been no justice and the victims and their families have not received any compensation from the state. During the government of Jamil Mahuad, the executive used the excuse that there was a lot of delinquency in Guayaquil to enforce a state of emergency for a large part of the term of the administration. The navy was charged with combatting delinquency and there were numerous allegations of human rights violations, with torture and unlawful entry into people's homes. There have also been claims that a death squad is operating in Guayaquil, where human rights organisations say a group of masked 'para-police' killed at least 20 supposed delinquents in the first few months of 1999.

17 July 1999 (Saturday) Jamil Mahuad today promised indigenous leaders he would freeze fuel and gas prices for a year at the level in force before the increase decreed on 1 July. With this agreement the indigenous abandoned their protests throughout the country.

Leaders of CONAIE and representatives of different areas of the country met Mahuad and ministers for more than nine hours in the government house, to draw up the agreement at 5 o'clock today. The indigenous made a series of demands, which the government accepted. An agreement was drawn up, which was signed by Mahuad, the government minister Vladimiro Alvarez Grau, the chancellor Benjamín Ortiz and the indigenous leaders Ricardo Ulcuango and Antonio Vargas.

As well the freeze on fuel and gas prices, the government agreed to set up round-table talks with the indigenous movement and other social sectors within two weeks. These would discuss the modernisation of the country without the new privatisations, the renegotiation of the foreign debt and the installation of US bases on Ecuadorian territory (see page 46).

The government agreed not to introduce any bills or issue any decrees on these matters before they had been discussed in the round-table talks. Mahuad ended the meeting by saying that the agreements demonstrated 'the government's concern to end the conflict between Ecuadorians'.

Ulcuango stated that the agreement was a victory for all the social movements, but questioned the fact that they could only get results by uprisings. 'Let us hope that the government is really concerned, that this not just another lie, and we don't have to have another uprising. It is not right that they only listen to us when our peoples come out of their communities to fight,' he said.

There was also an agreement on a subsidy for electricity consumption in indigenous areas, special treatment for street traders so that they would not have to pay VAT on sales below a figure to be determined, compensation for the wounded and families of those who had died in the protests, and the creation of a Fund for Indigenous Development.

Mahuad agreed to unfreeze the bank accounts of non-profit social and non-governmental organisations, frozen since 11 March.

'In the negotiations we demonstrated indigenous participation. There were representatives from different regions, not just the leaders, and thus we demonstrated our unity,' said Ulcuango.

Yesterday the Ecuadorian single-chamber parliament approved an amnesty for people imprisoned during the protest, but by today they had not been released.

On Friday afternoon lorry drivers agreed to end their strike after the government said it would renegotiate their debts. The taxi drivers, however, announced that they would continue on strike because the agreement reached by the other transport workers did not represent the wishes of the rank and file. After this morning's agreement between the indigenous and the government, Pedro Alava, president of the taxi drivers' union, organised the victory parade with 4,000 cars driving through Quito.

'This was our way of saying thank you for the struggle of the indigenous people who came here to fight for all of us and achieved something the transport leaders were unable to achieve,' he said.

EPILOGUE TO THE JULY 1999 UPRISING –
A MOVEMENT SHOWS ITS TRUE COLOURS
19 July 1999

The past few weeks have shown that Ecuador's indigenous movement is the only popular sector capable of winning real gains by protest in a country where the trades unions are not representative.

No one imagined that Jamil Mahuad's government would give way on issues such as the year-long freeze on fuel and gas prices. However, the CONAIE-organised uprising forced the government to back down.

The 1990 uprising was the starting point for this new phase in which the indigenous movement, regarded as the best organised in America, moved on from being a social protagonist to political protagonist. Then, the ethnic element and the demand for a pluri-national Ecuador were factors uniting the different indigenous nations. But CONAIE decided to go further, and sought alliances with other social and independent trades unions to create the Pachakutik Movement.

'The importance of Pachakutik is that it represents the social movements without the sponsorship of any political party. This was the factor that united both the Indian and non-Indian peoples of the country round an alternative political project,' says indigenous leader Luis Macas.

Their initial strength looked as if it were foundering on differences between different indigenous leaders. Some favoured agreements with officialdom to attain the vice-presidency of the legislative parliament or leadership of the Nations and Peoples of Ecuador – an autonomous organisation but with links to the executive, and one which seems to have become increasingly dependent on the government in recent months.

On the other hand, ECUARUNARI, a member organisation of CONAIE, consisting of people from the Sierra of Quechua nationality, the largest 'nation', wanted to distance themselves from the

government and challenge its economic policy.[21]

With Ricardo Ulcuango as their president, ECUARUNARI also demanded the resignation of the indigenous member of parliament Nina Pacari from the vice-presidency of the parliament, because they considered the office had been obtained by 'agreement with the parliamentary block of a government with whom they were in total disagreement'.

In June the CONAIE national assembly accepted ECUARUNARI's proposals and the uprising, announced to coincide with the beginning of the debate on the new privatisation bill, began on 6 July. It was precipitated by the rise in fuel prices decreed on 1 July and the general strike of taxi drivers called on 5 July.

Meanwhile, indigenous from the Sierra took over cities, drinking water plants, electricity stations and radio and television stations to demand the reduction of fuel prices and the shelving of the privatisation bill. The indigenous of Amazonia believed they would achieve more by not confronting the government, and did not join the protests.

In Quito, the indigenous held an assembly which they asked Nina Pacari not to take part in

---

[21] The Confederation of Peoples of the Quechua Nation of Ecudaor (ECUARUNARI) brings together all the Quechua peoples. It is the most important of the regional organisations which form CONAIE, because the Quechua are the most numerous, with more than 3 million people. For this reason its president is almost as important as the leader of CONAIE. At ECUARUNARI's 15th Congress in April 2000 official delegates attended from the Quechua peoples as well as representatives from the non-indigenous peasant sectors and from affiliated organisations in the Sierra. Eduardo Remache was elected president. The former president of ECUARUNARI, Ricardo Ulcuango, was elected president of CONAIE in September 1999.

until the communities gathered in Quito had reached an agreement with the government. They also asked the political parties not to try to make political gains from their movement.

After the executive refused to talk with them they marched towards the government house. When they got near it they were intercepted by police who told them that Mahuad would receive 20 leaders and would send a vehicle to fetch them. Everyone shouted that representatives of all the communities present should go to the meeting, amounting to about 500, or that Mahuad should come to meet them. After nine hours of talks, it was 70 indigenous, including CONAIE and ECUARUNARI leaders and representatives of the provinces, who reached an agreement with the government early on Saturday morning, and lifted the protest.

According to different polls, until June CONAIE was the third most credible institution in Ecuador, with 14 per cent, after the Catholic church and the armed forces, and above the media, which had been rapidly dropping in the polls over the last year. Some analysts say the results that the indigenous won through the uprising, the support from different sectors, and the military repression may mean that CONAIE now has greater credibility than the armed forces.

MAURICIO USHIÑA

Ecuador, the United States and Colombia

A SOVEREIGN BASE – OF THE UNITED STATES
27 July 1999

The installation of a US military base in the port of Manta, on Ecuador's Pacific coast, is supported by Jamil Mahuad's government and opposed by the indigenous movement, parts of the Catholic church and human rights groups.

The Ecuadorian government defends siting the base in this port, arguing that it will be a back-up for its own armed forces. Last May it sanctioned the first operations of US aeroplanes in the region.

The imminent need for a new site for the military forces posted at the Panama Canal over the past century, has led the US government to speed up the transfer of its bases to Ecuador, and to Aruba and Curazao in the Caribbean. The United States will hand over the canal to the Panama government on 31 December, according to the treaty signed in 1977 by the then presidents, Jimmy Carter and Omar Torrijos.[22]

Spokespersons for the indigenous and other social movements said they will oppose the installation of the military base at round-table talks with the government due to begin next week. The government agreed to these talks in the accord it signed with CONAIE to put an end to the two-week uprising by the communities earlier this month.

The government said it would not introduce any bill or issue any decrees relating to privatisation, the foreign debt or the US presence at Manta before discussing them, so the procedures relating to the installation of the base have been suspended.

Monsignor Luis Alberto Luna Tobar, archbishop of Cuenca, said the base at Manta is 'a very grave affront to our liberty, our autonomy, and above all, our sovereignty'.

Defence minister, retired general José Gallardo, sees the US military presence as a back-up for the Ecuadorian armed forces against possible Colombian guerrilla incursions. Gallardo stated that the armed forces were 'profoundly concerned' by the presence of insurgents from the Colombian Armed Revolutionary Forces (FARC) and by the coca plantations in the border region of Puntamayo.

The Ecumenical Commission for Human Rights fears that the strongly militaristic emphasis placed on combating drugs traffic and the Colombian guerrillas will involve Ecuador in continental strategies that 'redefine the role of the national armies in the region'.

The Commission says the possible environmental impact of the military base must be taken into account. 'We do not know what type or quantity of explosive and other contaminating elements might be used in military bases and in firing practice, or the costs of the technology to clean up these areas properly,' said the organisation.

In 1998 the Pentagon planned to carry out 186 military operations in the region, of which 21 were to be in Ecuador. That same year, Ecuadorian and US military took part in exercises against drugs trafficking in the Amazon jungle. In 2000 the armed forces of both countries were jointly constructing an anti-drugs camp, and three more have been announced for Amazonia and seven for other regions in the country.

Ecuadorian historian Jorge Nuñez says Washington's interest in territorial concessions and facilities in Ecuador is not new. ' In 1812 the US established a first naval base on the Galapagos Islands to attack English ships in the Pacific. Later, they tried to procure the sale or lease of the islands. During the Second World War they built a

---

[22] The Panama Canal was duly handed back to Panama at the end of 1999.

base in the archipelago, which they abandoned in 1946,' said Nuñez.

In 1986 there were demonstrations against the presence in the country of general John Galvin, then chief of the US southern command, and against the reported agreement between the two countries' armed forces to set up a School of the Americas[23] and install military bases. In 1987, during the presidency of León Febres Cordero, 6,900 US soldiers, under the southern command, formed Task Force 1169, which for six months took part in the military operation called Opening

Routes in the Amazon province of Napo.

Argentine Nobel peace prize-winner, Adolfo Pérez Esquivel, said in a letter published on Thursday that a possible intervention of the United States in Colombia, 'would set the horizon on fire in Latin America'.

[23] The School of the Americas, run by the US military, was responsible for training many of the military personnel involved in dictatorships in Latin America in the 1970s and 1980s.

THE COLOMBIAN FACTOR
6 August 1999

A contingent of the special operations forces of the US southern command is in the Amazon region of Ecuador and Peru, on the two countries' frontier with Colombia.

From the naval base of Iquitos in Peru, and the Coca Jungle School in Ecuador, units equipped with advanced war-intelligence technology are mobilising to neutralise incursions by Colombian guerrillas and drugs traffickers. The two bases, financed by the US defence department, began operating in March, when the Ecuadorian and Peruvian armies withdrew the troops they had been deploying in the now-resolved border conflict on the northern frontier.

General Barry McCaffrey, director of the US National Policy Office for the Control of Drugs, said last week in Ecuador that Washington will not intervene militarily in Colombia. Thus McCaffrey denied the report in the Lima daily paper *La Republica* that the United States was promoting the intervention of Ecuadorian and Peruvian troops in the Colombian conflict.

According to the version denied by McCaffrey, this plan was said to have been presented the previous month to the Peruvian government's presidential security adviser, Vladimiro Montesinos.

But the White House official did not reply when he was asked at a press conference whether the crash two weeks ago of the US military RC-7B aircraft on the Colombia-Ecuador frontier did not prove US covert intervention in Colombia. Within a few hours of the crash 24 aeroplanes were mobilised from Ecuadorian Amazonia to help in the search for the aircraft, which had crashed into a hill, according to *The Miami Herald*.

The US special operations forces assist the Ecuadorian and Peruvian military in combined operations and in planning and with training equipment, the US defence department told the US congress in April. The plan is to intercept communications by traffickers and the left-wing Colombian Armed Revolutionary Forces (FARC), according to the defence department.

Most of the US troops in Ecuador and Peru are pilots, qualified to operate radar stations and interpret images from multi-spectral cameras like those produced by the RC-7B aircraft used for identifying objects in the jungle.

General Carlos Mendoza, chief of the joint command of Ecuador's armed forces, denied that Ecuador was going to participate in operations against the Colombian guerrillas, although he admitted that there are 5,000 soldiers on the frontier to prevent the entry of Colombian rebels.

Three weeks days before the RC-7B accident, Ecuadorian and US troops carried out Operation Sucumb'os, to eliminate two FARC training camps in Ecuador.

The Peruvian naval base of Iquitos has a permanent group of 33 US military advisers, who rotate every 90 days, said *El Espectador*. Brazilian, Colombian and Ecuadorian military are being trained in jungle combat techniques in Coca, Ecuador, in a programme sponsored by the US defence department.

Ecuador's defence minister, José Gallardo, denied that the Coca base was a platform for a possible military intervention in Colombia. He said that officers from many countries are being trained there because of the centre's international prestige. 'There is nothing mysterious about it. It is a common interchange between the armed forces of different countries,' said Gallardo.

In Ecuador, McCaffrey spoke with president Jamil Mahuad and military chiefs about using the airbase of the port of Manta, where the United States has an Advanced Information Post for Regional Anti-drug Operations.

If the agreement for the United States to use the Manta base goes through, 200 men would arrive, comprising Drug Enforcement Agency agents, members of the coastal services and soldiers.

THE FARC, THE COLOMBIAN CONFLICT AND ECUADOR
May 2000

The Armed Revolutionary Forces of Colombia (FARC) is the largest and most powerful guerrilla organisation in Colombia, with more than 15,000 members, huge economic clout and massive influence over much of the country's population. In May 2000 it was taking part in peace talks with the Colombian government of Andrés Pastrana, although its confrontations with the army and police were intensifying.

Various political and social sectors in Ecuador and Colombia are afraid that the Colombian conflict might spill into Ecuadorian territory, resulting in a Kosovo-style air war. The fear arises from the implementation of the so-called Colombia Plan, a US$7.5 billion package of international economic aid, supposedly earmarked for combating drugs-trafficking, which according to some US analysts could trap the United States in a 'South American Vietnam'. The package is made up of US$4 billion from the Colombian government, US$1.6 billion from the US government, US$1 billion from the European Union and the rest from international organisations. The Colombian daily paper *El Colombiano* has stated that out of every US$1,000 dollars of US aid, US$700 are for military co-operation.

One of the most important components of the aid programme, called Push to the South of Colombia, involves US$600 million dollars to train two special anti-drugs battalions. It will provide 30 Blackhawk helicopters and 33 Huey helicopters in order to give them access to the remote jungles where coca is produced. A spokesman for the FARC, Raúl Reyes, said that the financial aid Washington had promised Pastrana to finance the Colombia Plan was a 'declaration of war'.

Ecuador's defence minister, Hugo Unda, has said that the intensification of the drugs war though the Colombia Plan could lead to the flooding of thousands of Colombian refugees into Ecuador, as well as drug-traffickers and guerrillas.

Most of the US aid for Colombia is for technology and combat weaponry to the Tres Esquinas base – an almost inaccessible military unit in the south of Colombia, amidst 77,000 hectares of coca cultivation.

Jorge Rojas, representative of the Committee for Human Rights and Displacement (CODHES) based in Bogotá, told the press that US aid will not resolve the drugs-trafficking problem, but will deepen and widen the conflict to other regions of Colombian Amazonia and even to neighbouring countries. 'This aid will extend the humanitarian crisis of forced displacement, increasing the number of refugees. It will directly affect Peru and Ecuador, which may become involved in the conflict. It will have an irreversible impact on the environment,' was Rojas' judgement.

He also said that various Colombian, Ecuadorian and Peruvian humanitarian organisations are working to create an 'observatory for civil society to keep watch on the Colombia Plan, and in particular, on US military aid'. The agency will produce specialised reports on the expansion of the conflict in Colombia and towards neighbouring countries; the real effects of US activity and crop-spraying in the drugs trade; the military impact on the displacement of people to Ecuador and on the deterioration of the environment.

Of the US$1.6 billion contributed by the United States to the Colombia Plan, US$88 million would go to Ecuador in what is seen as a sweetener for becoming involved in the plan.

According to some press reports, Ecuador has been assigned intelligence and surveillance functions in its territory, but when the plan is operating more fully, Ecuador might become involved in a war in which all the fighting forces active within Colombia will take part.

Some observers say the financial aid promised by the United States to the new Ecuadorean government, which took office on 22 January after the overthrow of ex-president Jamil Mahuad is conditional on active participation in the Colombia Plan.

In February 2000, the first to arrive in Ecuador was the secretary for political affairs, Thomas Pickering, who promised president Gustavo Noboa financial aid and talked about 'the need for closer collaboration in the region' to combat drugs trafficking. He also analysed the impact of drugs trafficking and the guerrillas on the country and US 'collaboration' to develop 'prevention' activities.

Martín Corena, commander of the FARC southern block with 2,500 men under him, has declared on television that if the Ecuadorian government continues supporting the United States from the Manta base, it will become a military target. According to press reports, the joint command of Ecuador's armed forces, who have knowledge of this 'warning', are concerned about the possibility of confrontations with the Colombian guerrillas.

People who live on the frontier between Ecuador and Colombia accept the presence of guerrillas who cross over to get food and combat gear as a form of 'non-traditional tourism', which brings in money. According to press reports, it is calculated that a high percentage of the population of Sucumb'os, a province on the frontier with Colombia, has direct or indirect relations with the guerrillas and the drugs trade.

Miguel Lluco, national co-ordinator of the Pachakutik Movement for Plurinational Unity, says Ecuador's agreement to the use of the Manta base by US ships and military involved it directly in a conflict which is becoming internationalised.

Until 1998, Ecuador was neutral in the internal conflicts of other countries, including Colombia, but this changed with the handing over of the Manta base to the United States.

According to unofficial sources, the United States has programmed the investment of about US$66 million for adapting the Manta base runway, in order to be able to carry out surveillance operations in the Andes region, covering Bolivia, Colombia, Peru and Venezuela.

In February 2000 defence minister Hugo Unda presented a report on the security of the Ecuador-Colombia frontier. He did not rule out the prospect of the Ecuadorian government shortly declaring a state of emergency in the area. Some analysts say that the reports of Colombian guerrillas in Ecuador are intended to create the conditions for US intervention in the region.

Debt, dollars, headaches and sweeteners

20 August 1999 The announcement of a moratorium on Ecuador's foreign debt until March 2000 has confirmed the the depth of the country's year-long financial crisis.

The step took many people by surprise although international economic analysts had been talking about the possibility for over a month. On 13 July the *Wall Street Journal* published a report warning that Ecuador could be the first country to go under after a Brady bonds re-structuring of its foreign debt. According to the paper, Ecuador was obliged to re-structure its Brady payments and this would drag down the whole model with it.

'Even though the re-structuring has been carried out by a small country,' it might call into doubt 'Latin America's capacity to overcome its

susceptibility to financial panic, which arrived here last year from Russia and East Asia,' said the New York daily.

If the panic generated by the Ecuadorian crisis results in the collapse of the Brady bonds, investors and holders of these documents might force larger debtors such as Argentina, Brazil and Venezuela to pay higher interest rates to protect their investments in Latin America, according to analysts.

IMF documents suggest that what worries its technical officers most in their negotiations to sign a letter of intent with Ecuador in the near future is the country's financial crisis and its growing burden of foreign debt in public finances.

Under a 'stand-by' agreement with the IMF, Ecuador could count on US$400 million to strengthen its balance of payments and US$500 million to begin restructuring its financial system.

Some economic analysts believe the Ecuadorian government should try to derive an advantage from the Brady bonds. The daily *El Comercio* asks whether it isn't morally justifiable to resort to whatever weapons one holds when the country has reached the point of either saving itself or collapsing. 'The Brady bonds are a bogeyman for debt holders. But they could become the Ecuadorian government's saving grace,' said the paper.

Ecuador's economic and monetary authorities denied that the country was about to declare a unilateral moratorium on debt payments. However, the explanations were somewhat contradictory. Modesto Correa, one of the directors of the Central Bank, said he did not know whether the finance minister, Ana Lucía Armijos, would take to her meeting with IMF representatives in Washington the proposal to defer payment of US$94 million worth of interest on Brady bonds, due on 31 August.

Correa attributed market nervousness to the fact that economic agents are well informed on the state of national accounts. 'We all know that, given the crisis, it is not easy to fulfil our debt obligations, but we will do everything possible to honour it,' he added. With reference to the payment due the following week, Correa explained that there was a 'technical delay' in the trusteeship of Brady debt, which allowed for the deferment of payment for 30 days from the date when it fell due.

President Jamil Mahuad said his government was seeking alternative solutions to the debt problem. 'We want it to be a decision that uses market mechanisms,' he said.

Ex-finance minister Pablo Concha said deferring payment of the bonds within a re-structuring of the debt is the only viable option, because this would release resources that are currently tied up. Concha calculated that Ecuador spends 54 per cent of its budget on debt payment and that next year this would rise to 60 per cent. He also explained that the financial impact of the volume of Brady bonds did not amount to even 1 per cent of all the documents circulating in the market. 'What Ecuador can re-negotiate is barely US$3 billion, that is to say, 0.3 per cent, insignificant in the markets,' he said.

US investment bank, Lehman Brothers, recommended that Ecuador should re-structure its foreign debt, 'in an organised way with the IMF and the Paris Club'. According to Lehmann Brothers, Ecuador should seek a reduction in the interest rate rather than a remission of the debt. 'The fiscal crisis and the service of the debt show that Ecuador cannot get out of the crisis by means of standard fiscal actions, because of the severity of its recession,' said the company.

This Saturday a new IMF mission arrived in the country, headed by John Thornton, to tie up the final details of the letter of intent that the government will sign before the end of August.

20 October 1999 (Wednesday) The uncontrollable fall of the *sucre* against the dollar is fuelling fears of hyperinflation.

The past two days have seen the dollar rise unexpectedly from 16,300 to 17,500 *sucres*. Between January and October, the *sucre* depreciated 154 per cent, while inflation for the period rose to 50 per cent.

Economists believe the rise in the dollar is caused by the purchase of US currency by banks in order to be ready next Wednesday for the unfreezing of savings accounts in dollars. The freeze affected US$2.5 billion belonging to 3.5 million Ecuadorians. After social protests in July, the government agreed with the indigenous movement to advance the unfreezing of currents accounts in *sucres* and savings accounts in dollars. Accounts in *sucres* have been unfrozen gradually since the agreement. A further US$200 million will be unfrozen next week.

The government attributed the rise in the dollar to parliament's failure to approve the budget for the year 2000, a pre-condition laid down by the IMF before releasing a loan of US$1.3 billion. The budget plan sent to parliament by president Jamil Mahuad is as high as US$4.4 billion, of which US$2.4 billion is for interest and capital repayments on Ecudaor's foreign debt.

The budget plan proposes to increase VAT from 10 to 15 per cent and reduce the threshold for paying individual income tax from US$500 to US$190 a month. It also proposes an increase in business tax from 15 to 25 per cent without taking the size of company into account.

Mahuad ruled out pacts with the right-wing parties, the Partido Social Cristiano (PSC, Christian Social Party) of the mayor of Guayaquil and former president León Febres Cordero and the Partido Roldosista Ecuatoriano (PRE) of former president Abdalá Bucaram who proposed the advance sale of oil to generate resources.

The government and centre-left parties insist that advance sale of oil would involve the sale not only of crude oil now being mined but also of reserves. The social-democratic Democratic Left (ID) of former president Rodrigo Borja (1988-92) agreed with a VAT increase but only of 2 per cent, while the Pachakutik

Movement did not agree with any of the proposed budget.

Both sectors demand a reduction in the percentage of the budget earmarked to pay the foreign debt from 54 to 30 per cent, and the redirecting of the difference into social spending.

Pablo Better, president of the Central Bank, said the Bank could not protect the sucre if there was no parliamentary political agreement on the budget and tax reform.

'With political speculation as to whether the budget will be approved or not, the dollar is rising. And the Central Bank is not intervening in the market,' he said.

According to Better, the price of the dollar should be set between 12,500 and 12,600 *sucres*, but the increase is produced by factors that cannot be controlled by monetary policy. 'If by the end of November we still do not have a definite approval of the agreement by the directors of the IMF, I see this as terrible for the country,' he said.

Better said that there was no alternative economic plan that could be applied if the budget proposed by the government was not approved. This would prevent a definitive agreement with the IMF.

Economic analyst Alberto Acosta disagreed with the view that the only way out for the budget was to raise VAT and that the only way out for Ecuador was the agreement with the IMF. 'If VAT is raised from 10 to 12 per cent, the treasury will get about US$120 million, less than the US$200 million a year we lose for oil that is not paid for by private oil companies, and much less than the US$240 million budget to cover future bank collapses,' said Acosta. 'We only have to see how the IMF handled the crisis in the Asian countries, in Russia and Brazil, to see how demagogically they weave hopes round this institution,' he added.[24]

Acosta said the government's proposed budget ran contrary to the logic behind the suspension of the servicing of Brady bonds, because 'it earmarks 54 per cent of expenditure for the debt'.

Some sectors questioned the fact that the government continues to bail out banks and then asks for a tax increase. In the past few weeks two banks have been rescued, which, according to the government, were not in danger of failing. The president of one was also president of the government's National Modernisation Council, which was in charge of privatising state enterprises.

Luis Maldonado, president of the Ecuadorian Federation of Exporters, said one of the worst aspects of the crisis was the irrational management of resources, which were paid out 'to an immoral, usurous bank'.

Some analysts say the lack of control over the dollar is one of the gravest symptoms of the economic crisis. 'The government appears to have opted to allow things to reach a point of no return as a way of forcing the country to accept the single government plan based on the agreement with the IMF,' said an editorial in the daily *Expreso de Guayaquil*.

Raul Mendizábal, president of the Pichincha Chamber of Small Commerce, said that if the dollar's upward tendency persisted, he could not rule out 'the imminent closure of about 22,000 small businesses at national level'. 'In every firm we have had to reduce staff by 50 per cent and this increases the problem of unemployment,' said Mendizábal.

In the midst of the crisis the bonanza in the world oil market has been the only thing that has given the country a fiscal breathing space, because oil has gone up from US$8 per barrel in March to US$22 per barrel.

22 October 1999 (Friday) The mayor of Quito, and businesses, have proposed the dissolution of parliament. The government party is accused of having received more than US$10 million from bankers for Jamil Mahuad's presidential campaign.

Meanwhile, the government, which last month announced a partial moratorium on Brady bond payments, also declared that it was unable to pay the Eurobonds which fell due today, and that these would be included in the restructuring of the foreign debt.

The Quito Chambers of Commerce and Industry, and other business institutions, blame parliament for the economic crisis for not accepting the tax increases proposed by the government in the budget reform for the year 2000. They claim this 'obstructionist' attitude, and the fact that it has not yet been possible to carry out the privatisations, demonstrate the 'inefficiency' of the legislators. The mayor of Quito, Roque Sevilla, has also declared that institutional order has broken down.

The leader of the Democratic Left, retired general Paco Moncayo, said he suspected that the attack on parliament was an attempt to divert attention from the accusations of corruption in money management made against various bankers in Mahuad's campaign. Moncayo wondered how a party that came into government with a campaign financed by banks could be independent of them.

In March before the imminent collapse of the Progress Bank, one of the biggest in the country, the government ordered the freezing for a year of 50 per cent of the balances of current and savings accounts above

[24] For an analysis of IMF policy and recent financial crises see David Woodward, *Time to Change the Prescription. A policy response to the Asian financial crisis*, London: CIIR 1999.

US$200, and the total freezing of deposits above US$500 in both current and term held in foreign currency. The freeze did not achieve much, because a month later the bank announced its collapse, and even though its president, Fernando Aspiazu, was accused of mismanaging funds, the government allowed the Central Bank to give it credit and begin a recovery process.

In July the government imprisoned Aspiazu. Many people thought this was for effect because it occurred when the demonstrations by indigenous and taxi drivers were intensifying, and after a severe repression of 15,000 indigenous who had entered Quito on a peaceful March. The banker was indicted for having collected the tax on his clients' bank transactions and not paid it over to the state. This had been revealed many months before but nothing had been done about it.

This week from prison the banker asked for accounts stating how the US$3.1 million, which he claimed to have contributed to Mahuad's electoral campaign, had been spent. This was a bombshell in the political arena.

According to Ecuadorian laws, after the elections the presidential candidates have to present a declaration of electoral expenses, with a statement of where the money came from, to the Supreme Electoral Tribunal.

The banker claimed that his contribution was missing from the declaration that the government party made to the tribunal. A week ago he showed proofs of the bank transfers in the name of Ramón Yulee, treasurer of the campaign and secretary to the presidency. Aspiazu set up a legal investigation to establish where this money, given for the campaign, had gone. He provided a list of bankers and firms who had also contributed.

Until a few days ago Alvaro Guerrero, president of the La Previsora Bank, which went bankrupt two weeks earlier and was taken over by a state bank, had been director of the National Council for Modernisation, which is in charge of carrying out the privatisations. Guillermo Lasso, from the Bank of Guayaquil, was governor of the coastal province of Guayas, nominated by the executive and economic minister. Nicolás Landes, president of the Banco Popular which also collapsed two weeks before and was saved by the government, left the country just days before the Courts began a case against him for irregularities in his bank. Medardo Cevallos, former ambassador to Mexico for Mahuad's government and a shareholder in Bancomex, another of the banks that collapsed, was also facing a court case. Another who had contributed was Javier Espinosa, president of the Quito Chamber of Commerce – one of the bodies demanding the dissolution of parliament – until two months ago when he became a member of the cabinet, first as development and currently as economy minister.

The businessmen demanding the dissolution of parliament agree with the government view that foreign exchange speculation, which drove up the dollar during the first three days of the week, was caused by parliament. 'Because parliament persisted in its obstructionist attitude, the time has come to think of applying the constitution and revoking its mandate to rule, on the grounds that it has not fulfilled its obligations and has encouraged acts of corruption, such as foreign exchange speculation,' they said in a communiqué.

Some analysts believed the speculation was provoked by the

banks going out to buy dollars. Last Wednesday, after the rise in the dollar, the superintendent of banks Jorge Guzmán met the bankers to analyse the crisis. On the following day, demand for the US currency fell, and so did its price. Analysts interpreted the decrease in speculation as a direct consequence of this meeting.

Pachakutik Movement member of parliament Antonio Poso said that the allegations by businessmen and the mayor were a campaign to discredit parliament. 'They want to blame parliament for a crisis caused by the government after it had spent more than US$2 billion dollars on saving 15 banks over the past year,' said Poso.

Meanwhile, the chief of the joint command of the armed forces, Carlos Mendoza, said he was concerned by the economic crisis, but ruled out a coup. But he pointed out the need for 'parliament and the executive to reach agreement'.

The moratoria on Eurobonds and Brady bonds appear to be the only government measures to have gained the support of the social movements. However, the latter question the contradiction between taking these measures and earmarking 54 per cent of the draft budget for the year 2000 for foreign debt repayment.

28 December 1999 (Tuesday)
A reform of the penal code initiated by president Jamil Mahuad will allow legal proceedings against Abdalá Bucaram for embezzlement to be quashed. The former president will be permitted to return to the country without facing charges.

Last week parliament approved the amendments to the penal code proposed by Mahuad. The new text lays down, with retroactive effect, that legal proceedings can only be brought through an indictment by a public prosecutor, and proceedings against former presidents must be authorised by the legislature.

The five legal actions against Bucaram were begun without an indictment by a public prosecutor and without authorisation from parliament. The former president and his advisers were accused of appropriating public funds valued at more than US$22 million during the period of Bucaram's government, between August 1996 and February 1997, when Parliament sacked him for 'mental incapacity to govern'.

The sacking was preceded by protest demonstrations in which millions of people took part. Bucaram eventually fled to Panama, where he is still living. Now the ex-president can return to the country without facing any charges.

A new penal code was approved by parliament in November of this year. There was provision for a delay of 18 months before it came into force, so that there would be time for the cases against Bucaram to be completed. Mahuad has used a partial veto to put before parliament an amendment providing for the revised penal code to come into force immediately and with retroactive effect.

Analysts held that these proposals were part of an exchange of favours between the government and Bucaram's Ecuadorian Roldosista Party (PRE). On two occasions opposition members left the chamber in order to make parliament inquorate and prevent the approval of the amendments proposed by the president. But in the last session before Christmas, the president of the parliament, Juan José Pons, modified the order of the day without previous warning and within two minutes the amendments to the code proposed by Mahuad were voted through.

Pons's manoeuvre caught many opposition members unawares. They did not have time to leave the parliamentary premises and foil the approval of the amendments by members of the ruling Popular Democratic Party and the PRE.

In the corridors of parliament, visibly annoyed, some members said the government had 'pulled a fast one'. The leader of the Democratic Left block, Paco Moncayo, said what had happened was wrong and destroyed parliament's credibility. José Cordero, president of the parliamentary Committee for Civil and Penal Affairs, was one of the three members on the government bench to vote against the amendments. He said he would resign from this bench to express his disagreement with the pact between his party and that of Bucaram.

Susan Klinkicht, a political analyst and columnist on the daily paper *Hoy de Quito* said the most serious issue was not Bucaram's return but the fact that

he was able to return 'without answering to the law for his acts of corruption'. 'We should remember what happened three years ago, when the population's indignation resulted in the biggest demonstration the country had ever seen, the sole purpose of which was to get rid of Bucaram from the government,' Klinkicht said.

According to the columnist, Ecuadorians 'feel ashamed' that the government has accepted 'Bucaram's imposition' in order to get the budget proposals through. 'President Mahuad, who has put great emphasis on the good impression he makes abroad can no longer be certain of enjoying such goodwill, because it is difficult for anyone to understand his motivations for such gross lack of ethics,' added Klinkicht.

In another surprise on the same day, the superintendent of banks, Jorge Guzmán, asked for a restriction order on the directors of the La Previsora Bank, which collapsed in October with its management being handed over to the state. The order prevents these directors from leaving the country until their responsibility in the collapse has been determined.

Among those indicated as possibly responsible for irregularities in the management of the La Previsora were Alvaro Guerrero and Alfredo Arizaga, president and vice-president of the bank when it collapsed. Arizaga is currently finance minister, and Guerrero was director of the National Council for Modernisation until a few days after the collapse of the bank.

Some analysts think the restriction order against Arizaga seeks to demonstrate that the government is combating corruption, and thus disprove accusations against it about the possible quashing of the charges against Bucaram.

Mahuad dollarises

4 January 2000 (Tuesday) The sharp fall of the *sucre* against the dollar brings with it the spectre of hyperinflation which the government plans to combat either by adopting free convertibility, as in Argentina, or by dollarising the Ecuadorian economy.

In the past two days the dollar's rise has been unexpectedly high, moving from 20,000 to 23,000 *sucres* per US$1. Although the Central Bank did not intervene directly, the authorities may have put pressure on the *bureaux de changes* to limit dealing, and some institutions ceased currency dealing altogether.

From December 1999 to January 2000, the *sucre* depreciated 164 per cent, while inflation hit 60 per cent. Exchange clerks and economic experts said the dollar was responding to high demand from economic agents, who were expecting the announcement of the government's monetary programme for the year 2000 over the next few days. The possibility that this programme would adopt free convertibility of the *sucre* or dollarisation was fuelling speculation in the US currency, provoking its rise.

But analysts also said the rise of the dollar was produced by the free issue of currency by the Central Bank to deal with the debts of banks taken over by the state.

A presidential source told Inter Press Service that president Jamil Mahuad was in agreement with adopting free convertibility if it had strong national support. 'The possibility of establishing convertibility was one of the central points raised at the meeting held yesterday by the president with his cabinet. However, they believe that at this time dollarisation would be a leap

in the dark because the conditions are not there to impose it,' said the source, who preferred not to be identified.

Defenders of dollarisation include right-wing political sectors, the Guayaquil business sector, most of the country's bankers, some Sierra businessmen, and the directors of multinational companies in Ecuador. According to them, dollarisation would stabilise the currency, improve conditions for Ecuador's participation in international trade, strengthen the weak national banking system and reduce the risk of inflation by requiring greater fiscal discipline.

But indigenous leaders and leaders of social, left and centre-left political movements, university representatives, small business people and some industrialists and bankers, consider that dollarisation would not be viable in a country like Ecuador, whose banking system is in a state of collapse. They say it would increase Ecuador's dependence on the external context.

Economic analyst, Andrés Hidalgo believes there is no magic formula to solve these problems. 'Any of these schemes is based on a type of fixed exchange and can only be sustained by keeping everything in perfect order. In the short term these schemes cannot be considered for Ecuador because there are problems such as the fiscal deficit and the debt, which must be resolved beforehand,' he said.

Technical workers in the main banks said the monetary policy measures applied in Argentina, Brazil, Bolivia and Peru were adopted when inflation had risen above 5,000 per cent, which is not the case in Ecuador.

Argentina's former economy minister Domingo Cavallo, advised the then president Abdalá Bucaram to adopt a free-convertibility plan similar to the Argentinean model, which established one-to-one parity between the *peso* and the dollar. But the proposal was strongly rejected in Ecuadorian political circles.

According to a poll in Argentina, 54 per cent of respondents believe that their personal situation had deteriorated as a result of convertibility, 16 per cent said it had improved and 30 per cent that it had made no difference.

The executive director of the Quito Chamber of Commerce, Armando Tomaselli, stressed that the price instability of the dollar could not be combated by a monetary and exchange policy but only by rational management of the country. 'All schemes work well when there is coherent economic management, but they cause problems when the authorities do not run the economy well,' he said. The most worrying problem at the moment is the issuing of currency to bail out banks. This has become an inflationary measure and a fundamental cause of the devaluation of the *sucre*, Tomaselli said.

Last week differences arose between the president of the Central Bank, Pablo Better, and Jorge Guzmán, superintendent of banks and president of the Agency for the Security of Deposits, which administers the 15 banks that have collapsed over the past 14 months. Better is opposed to the continued issue of currency, but Guzmán considers it is the only way to pay off the debts of the financial bodies. Guzmán said that the principal source of finance for the Agency for the Security of Deposits should be the sale of the rescued banks' assets, which amount to nearly US$4 billion, but that this will take time. And 'it is absurd to tell the depositors to wait for the assets to be sold before they can get their money back.'

7 January 2000 (Friday) The Confederation of Indigenous Nations of Ecuador (CONAIE) has announced an indefinite national protest, to start on Saturday 15 January until president Jamil Mahuad resigns, parliament is dissolved and members of the supreme court of justice are removed.

CONAIE proposes to form 'a patriotic government of national unity', in which the armed forces, the social sectors and independent professionals will participate.

The protest will take place amid the political and economic instability caused by the devaluation of the sucre by 30 per cent during the first week of the year, and rumours of a possible coup by the military. Some 92 per cent of the population now rejects the government.

The indigenous protest would be joined by transport workers and other trade union and peasant sectors.

Indigenous leader Miguel Lluco said Ecuadorians had lost patience with the government's failure to resolve the country's problems. 'The indigenous movement and other social sectors have given the president many opportunities, suggesting solutions which could have worked and seeking dialogue, but he would never listen to us,' said Lluco.

For example, he said, after the protests of July 1999, round-table talks had been set up between the social movements and the government to seek joint solutions to political, economic and social problems, but the authorities never kept their promises. Among government betrayals, Lluco mentioned the permission given for the installation of the US military base at Manta without any public debate; the failure to tax bank utilities, luxury vehicles and capital gains in order to shift the tax burden onto the richest; and the failure to reduce foreign debt payments which currently represent 54 per cent of the state budget. 'The country was falling to pieces and the government continued giving its last *sucres* to corrupt bankers. The reason for this becomes plain now that it is known that it was these bankers who financed the president's electoral campaign,' he said.

Lluco declared that the indigenous movement is not interested in just a change of names, 'because this won't change anything, which is what happened when Abdalá Bucaram was sacked and Fabián Alarcón took over as president'. Alarcón at the time was president of the parliament. 'We do not believe in anybody, which is why the members of parliament must also go home, because apart from a few exceptions they also contributed to letting the crisis get worse. It's the same with the supreme court, which is subject to constant corruption,' he said.

To take the place of parliament, on Wednesday 12 January the National Parliament of the Peoples of Ecuador will be set up in Quito. It will consist of delegates sent by indigenous, workers, peasants, professionals, religious and small businesses from all over the country. 'The parliament will work out and present a plan of changes to be made to get the country out of its crisis. It will be the preamble to a new indigenous and popular uprising,' said Lluco. He also said that the social movements 'will not be a ladder to become vice-president or president of parliament, as some right-wing sectors want.'

In recent weeks the indigenous leaders have held meetings with senior officers in the armed forces, who are in agreement with their proposal.

A soldier watches as indigenous advance towards Quito, January 2000.

However, there are conflicting views within the army about the role it should play. One sector supports the indigenous movement's proposal, another wants Mahuad to finish his term, and a third supports the resignation of the president so that vice-president Gustavo Noboa can take over, as happened formerly with Rodrigo Borja (1988-92) and León Febres Cordero (1984-88).

Ecuador's armed forces enjoy a high standing among the population because of their nationalist position, their support work for the poorest social sectors and because they have not taken part in the sorts of human rights violations that have happened in the southern cone of Latin America.[25]

In July 1999, after the arrival of thousands of indigenous on a peaceful march to Quito, the government ordered the army to employ repressive tactics, which was out of character for the army and dented its popularity. The military, which was widely condemned for behaving in this way, later gave the government an ultimatum to reach agreement with the indigenous, saying that the army was not prepared to carry out any more repression. However, the military was put on the spot again this year when they failed to oppose the installation of a US base in the port of Manta.

This week, the trades unions grouped in the Single Workers' Front, teachers and other sectors linked to the left-wing Popular Democratic Movement (MPD) staged demonstrations but did not gain broad popular support. Yet as soon as the protests were announced, Mahuad declared a state of emergency and suspended all individual civil rights.

Some analysts believe the emergency gives the government the chance to declare the free convertibility of the *sucre*. But no measures have yet been taken because of serious disagreements within the economic team between the supporters and opponents of free convertibility. Although dollarisation was said to have been practically ruled out because of its high social costs, a

[25] The Ecuadorian army, the most powerful and numerous of the armed forces, has been involved with the indigenous communities and with the rural poor, supporting the construction of schools, roads and development projects. It gained respect for its handling of the conflict between Peru and Ecuador. In Ecuador the police are considered worse human rights violators. Within the forces there are differences between the army (more progressive and regionally linked to the Sierra) and the navy (linked more closely with the right and Guayaquil). In recent years the armed forces have played arbiter to democracy – in February 1997 when congress dismissed Abdalá Bucarám, and again in January 2000 when the commanders struck a blow in favour of Gustavo Noboa. The majority of the officers and troops who supported the 21 January uprising are at loggerheads with their commanders. Similarly there is a deep rift between the navy and army. The possibility of future confrontation cannot be ruled out. Gustavo Noboa, who at first opposed amnesty for those who took part in the rebellion, subsequently sent to congress a request for amnesty, believing this would pacify the military. There were fears that the social tensions brought about by economic hardships, and which dollarisation might exacerbate, could finally explode in June 2000, when the government was to announce new economic adjustment measures so as to comply with the conditions of the letter of intent signed in April 2000 with the International Monetary Fund. This, added to the internal crisis in the military, the deepening of regional differences between Quito and Guyaquil, and the Colombian conflict, which threatens to become regional, could be pushing Ecuador towards civil war.

government source said that with Mahuad you can never tell.

The Christian Social Party (PSC), the largest right-wing force outside the government and with strong support on the coast, is pressing for increased autonomy for the province of Guayas. The business sectors in this province, which include the large exporters, are pressing for dollarisation. And it now seems clear that the rise in the dollar was caused by speculation in the US currency by coastal exporters and some bankers.

Businessmen, bankers and the PSC appear to want Mahuad gone, so that the vice-president Gustavo Noboa can take over and implement drastic structural adjustment, step up privatisations and strengthen the neoliberal model. The idea is that something similar should happen as occurred with the former president of Argentina, Raúl Alfonsín.[26]

Meanwhile, Mahuad intends to turn the tables by forming a coalition with Bucaram's Roldosista party. He hope that this will win approval for the legal reforms necessary to privatise hydrocarbons, electricity, telecommunications, social security and basic education.

In a message from Panama, Bucaram announced his support for Mahuad and said that he would be returning to Ecuador in February.

[26] Alfonsín handed over the presidency to Carlos Menem in 1989, months before the specified date, because of hyper-inflation of more than 5,000 per cent per year. Inflation may have been due in large part to speculation by industry and the financial sector, which were pushing for Alfonsín's Radical Civic Union party to lose the elections, and for Alfonsín to hand over immediately to Menem who would implement neoliberal economic measures and privatisations.

9 January 2000 (Sunday) President Jamil Mahuad has responded to the crisis in Ecuador by dollarising the economy and asking his ministers to resign so that he can reform his cabinet. But he has been unable to silence calls for his resignation.

'After two months of analysis, meetings and listening to experts, I have reached the conclusion that dollarisation is a suitable and necessary system for Ecuador,' Mahuad said in a message broadcast today on national radio and television.

The new programme is to be implemented by the Central Bank, an autonomous body with directors elected by parliament. But the measure is opposed by most of the directors and the president of the bank himself, Pablo Better, who announced that he would not resign.

As a result, Mahuad summoned an extraordinary session of parliament for this Tuesday, with the sole purpose of raising the question of sacking the Central Bank's directors. The government said it can count on the necessary parliamentary majority to name new directors who are in line with its policy, because it is assured of

'this does not benefit the people, because we indigenous barely know the colour of dollars'

both the votes of the ruling DP and those of the Roldosistas.

Mahuad indicated that the pact with the Roldosistas would also enable him to get laws approved in order to introduce constitutional reforms allowing for the privatisation of oil, electricity, telecommunications and social security.

The coalition would be joined by the PSC, fervent advocates of dollarisation, even though its leaders believe it would be better for Mahuad to resign and dollarisation to be introduced by the vice-president.

The dollarisation plan involves the Central Bank using its liquid monetary reserves of US$500 million to replace the local currency, the *sucre*, in circulation. The Central Bank would cease to issue currency and would exchange all the existing *sucres* for dollars in its reserve, at a rate of 25,000 *sucres* per US$1. Then, without having any reserve currency at its disposal, the Central Bank would cease to be a currency-issuing body and become an agent for the restructuring of the country's banking and fiscal reorganisation. Once this has happened, the *sucre* will disappear because goods, services and anything traded will have a value in dollars. Wages will also be paid in dollars, without any increase.

Implementation of the new monetary scheme requires not only the consent of the Central Bank but also constitutional reforms that allow for the change in the currency. There will also have to be a change in the laws regulating the monetary system, financial institutions and the tax system to adapt them to dollarisation.

Finance minister, Alfredo Arizaga, ex vice-president of the La Previsora Bank, managed by the state since its collapse last year, said the process of replacing the *sucre* by the dollar would be a gradual one.

President Mahuad explained that dollarisation would make it possible to bring down inflation 'to international levels of 10 per cent or less' per year, which would eliminate the spectre of hyperinflation which reared up last week with the 30 per cent depreciation of the *sucre* against the dollar.

Ricardo Ulcuango, vice-president of CONAIE, said dollarisation is not appropriate for Ecuador, which does not have dollars but devalued *sucres*. He added that recently the government had allowed the dollar to rise to 25,000 *sucres* in order to introduce dollarisation. He said dollarisation is a desperate measure by the government to regain the support of businessmen and industrialists, who are the ones pressing for dollarisation. 'It is obvious that an agreement has been reached with big business, but this does not benefit the people, because we indigenous barely know the colour of dollars,' he said. Ulcuango said the Central Bank is autonomous, so the government cannot force it to adopt a decision.

Mahuad's announcement also limited the return of bank deposits frozen in March 1999. The banks can return the money belonging to those who have deposits under US$4,000. But those who have bigger balances will have to wait until March 2006 and 2009.

In banks which collapsed and were taken over by the state the refund will be in the form of official bonds, which can be traded on the stock market. According to experts this will represent a loss for savers because the bonds will be set at a much lower rate.

The package of economic measures announced by the president coincides with the views of the business chambers of the coast and the Sierra and the financial sector, whose representatives were pleased.

The president of the Quito Chamber of Commerce, Andrés Pérez, declared that the measures 'are important, not only to deal with the crisis that is smothering us, but to achieve the growth and well-being to which society aspires'. Pérez welcomed the fact that the government had finally shown firm leadership on key matters for the country, although he regretted it had not done so much earlier.

Instead of calming the social movements, president Mahuad's announcement added fuel to the fire. The mobilisation of the indigenous and the protest by different social and trade union sectors throughout the country, originally announced for next Saturday, was brought forward. This week the country will be paralysed with road blocks and other actions.

GM FOOD BLOCKADE
10 January 2000

Ecuadorian activists and farmers have intercepted a US ship before it docked at the port of Guayaquil, to prevent it unloading a cargo of 30,000 tonnes of genetically modified (GM) soya.

Last Tuesday 50 activists of the environmental organisation Ecological Action and members of the National Farmworkers' Committee took out two small craft to intercept the ship 'Frina', board her and prevent her from continuing her journey into port. Other environmentalists went to the port authorities, together with the ombudsman, Hernán Ulloa, and a civil judge, to demand that the ship should not be allowed to enter the port. The port authorities complied with their request.

The judge asked researchers at the Izquieta Pérez Biological Institute to analyse samples of the product to determine whether to allow the soya, destined for animal feed, to enter. The environmentalists declared that meat from animals fed on GM products represents health risks to consumers.

Ecological Action had been informed by US non-governmental organisations about the genetic modification of the soya transported by the 'Frina'. Now it expects that, once the analysis has been done, the ship's cargo will be incinerated or sent back to its port of origin.

'We hope there will be no corruption and the law will be kept that forbids the entry of GM foods into the country,' said Jorge Loor, director of the National Peasant Co-ordinating Committee and a member of the Parliament of the Peoples of Ecuador which will be set up tomorrow in Quito.

Genetic manipulation of the composition of animal or vegetable products seeks to increase their nutritional value, their resistance to disease and their shelf-life. Biologist Elizabeth Bravo of Ecological Action, says GM products are new and no one, not even the companies that make them, can predict their effects. 'The possible effects on human health and the environment are unpredictable,' said Bravo. She also warned of the socio-economic consequences of these products. 'Peasants will be obliged to obtain [GM] seeds, in order not to lose out to commercial competition,' she explained. 'Who will guarantee that the new seeds are good?' she wondered.

Most commercial GM products are foods, seeds and agricultural and medical consumables developed by multinational companies, chief among which are the US company Monsanto and the Swiss company Noartis. Their principal products are soya, tomatoes, potatoes, tobacco, cotton and maize resistant to herbicides and diseases.

The journal *Tribuna del Consumidor* warned a few months ago that GM products might be entering Ecuador undetected because they are not labelled as such.

Bravo also says soya imported from Argentina could be genetically modified. 'Even though Ecuador imports little soya, 80 per cent that comes from abroad comes from Argentina. No one can guarantee to date that it is not genetically modified, like most of the soya produced in that country,' Bravo said.

According to Ecological Action, potatoes imported from the United States for fast food restaurants of US origin could be genetically modified, as well as edible oils and some primary materials used in chicken feed.

The Ecuadorian constitution approved in November 1997 entrusted regulation of the import of GM products to the law. The constitutional rule can only be put into practice when a complementary law has been approved by parliament or by executive decree.

Participants in the First Andean Meeting on Biosecurity, in Quito last June, exhorted the countries of the Andean community to agree on safety mechanisms for GM products. Experts in biosecurity, representatives of the governments of Bolivia, Colombia, Ecuador, Cuba and Venezuela and UNESCO, warned at the same meeting that those taking the decisions on GM products did not have the necessary training to deal with the matter. The Latin American authorities, 'who decide on the introduction, use and management of living organisms modified by techniques of biotechnology need better training,' declared Arvelio Garc'a Rivas of UNESCO (United Nations Education, Science and Culture Organisation).

Santiago Carrasco, of the Ecuador National Secretariat for Science and Technology, said it was necessary to create of culture of biosecurity for the Andean region. The environmentalists gave as an example of the risks of GM agricultural produces the case of GM maize pollen, Bt, which researchers at Cornell University, New York, proved kills the larvae of the monarch butterfly. The studies sounded the alarm on the effects of pollen spread from the growing fields towards adjacent natural areas in the United States, Canada, Argentina and Spain, where this type of maize is produced and sold.

Peasant leader Jorge Loor believes the introduction of GM seeds is yet another error of Mahuad's government and 'yet another imposition by companies whose only interest is profit without caring how it affects the peasants'.

Rescuing democracy

11 January 2000 (Tuesday) The Peoples' Parliament, consisting of 330 representatives from the indigenous and civil society was set up today in the capital Quito to work out an alternative plan of government, while president Jamil Mahuad proceeds to demolish obstacles to his projected dollarisation of the economy.

Indigenous leader Miguel Lluco says the indigenous will work out economic, judicial and legislative guidelines and set up a participative model which will be the essence of democracy. 'Nobody believes in the current democracy. So we must rescue participation by civil society from below and restore to Ecuador the democracy it has been robbed of by right-wing political parties and unscrupulous bankers,' he said.

Lluco said the People's Parliament will speak against the dollarisation and privatisations which the government intends to implement, 'because they only benefit bankers and agro-exporters, who are the ones in Ecuador who have dollars'. 'It was the bankers who gave money for Mahuad's electoral campaign. He rewarded them by paying out US$2 billion to save their banks. Now he is going to dollarise so that they will continue to benefit. This is his way of rewarding those who gained him the presidency,' he said.

Silvia Vega, of the Women's Political Committee, maintained that by dollarisation the president 'has declared war on the people,' and pointed out that the alternative parliament does not recognise the three powers of the state. The Peoples' Parliament, made up of different social sectors from the indigenous to businessmen and professionals, has proposed the establishment of a new

form of administration led by a coalition government, a council of state, a national parliament and provincial parliaments.

Antonio Vargas, president of CONAIE, said at his inauguration as vice-president of the People's Parliament that the national indigenous uprising planned for this Saturday will start in the provinces.

The leader insisted that the indigenous 'will fight to the last until Mahuad, his cabinet, members of parliament and members of the court of justice all go home'. The Peoples' Parliament will sit indefinitely during the popular mobilisations.

On Monday, Guayaquil was besieged by transport workers demanding that their debts in dollars should be converted into *sucres* before the economy is dollarised.

Meanwhile, Mahuad has managed to unite all the right-wing political sectors and the financial and business sectors behind his dollarisation plan. This is the first time he has achieved this. He has gained the removal of the three principal authorities in the Central Bank who were opposed to his economic plan, including the bank's president, Pablo Better. Thus he has removed nearly all the legal obstacles to dollarisation.

In the next few days the single chamber national parliament is to approve various constitutional reforms to expedite the application of the new monetary system. Mahuad can count on the support of his Popular Democracy (DP) party, the right-wing Christian Social Party (PSC) with whom he governed in coalition for the first few months of his term before distancing himself from them, and the populist Roldosista (PRE) party of former president Abdalá Bucaram. Government spokespeople say this alliance will be enough to achieve the constitutional reforms required by dollarisation, which is opposed by the Pachakutik Movement, the Democratic Left (ID) and the MPD.

Mahuad says his government and the Central Bank hold enough dollars to exchange all the *sucres* in circulation. In a message broadcast on radio and television last Sunday, the president explained that dollarisation would be at a fixed rate of 25,000 *sucres*.

Meanwhile, the IMF announced it is sending a technical mission to Quito with the aim of assisting the Ecuadorian government to adapt its fiscal and banking strategies to the planned dollarisation. 'Once the appropriate measures have been identified, the IMF is prepared to work with the Ecuadorian authorities in support of its economic programme,' said Michel Camdessus, IMF executive director.

According to a poll by the firm Market, that happened to be published on Monday, a day after Mahuad's announcement, 58 per cent of the population approves Mahuad's proposal, whereas 41 per cent are against it.

Miguel Lluco said this poll was not very reliable because 'the owner of the firm Market, Blasco Peñaherrera, had been running a campaign in favour of dollarisation for the last few weeks'.

The socialist member of parliament and former vice-president of Ecuador, León Roldós Aguilera, said dollarisation had been in preparation for a long time.

Roldós Aguilera added, 'The impression is they pushed the dollar up. You have only to look who bought currency during this period. They were doing the deal of the century because now it is worth 30 per cent more.'

Miguel Lluco agreed with Roldós that it was no accident that weeks before the announcement of dollarisation, a campaign was launched to discredit the president of the Central Bank for opposing the measure. 'Today the Christian Social Party announced that it will bring a legal case against Pablo Better "for the damage he has done to the national economy in not adopting measures to halt the escalation of the dollar", which provides a basis for our suspicion that there was a plot to dollarise,' argued Lluco.

12 January 2000 (Wednesday)
CONAIE has announced that it will take power in 15 to 20 days and has told international organisations to watch what happens during the uprising of indigenous peoples, which will begin next Saturday.

The archbishop of Cuenca, Luis Alberto Luna Tobar, who was unanimously chosen as president of the alternative 'people's parliament', declared that the assembly 'will be a more effective weapon for the people to combat lies, corruption and falsehood'. The 'peoples' parliament' resolved to assume full powers in the political, economic, administrative and judicial spheres and called the whole country to civil disobedience.

Antonio Vargas, president of CONAIE, said that this popular parliament – of which he is vice-president – would be the real national parliament. It will elect a Junta of National Salvation, which will replace the government of Jamil Mahuad, and it will establish a system of 'popular justice'.

Vargas said that all the organisations of civil society represented in this indigenous-popular parliament are in all-out civil disobedience. He said the social movements are ready to 'take power'. 'The people will govern the country from here in 8, 15 or 20 days time,' said the indigenous leader. He stated that Ecuadorians 'have total sovereignty to demand the removal of the three powers of the state,' and called on the armed forces and police 'to unite with the movement'.

Before the National Parliament of the Peoples was established, CONAIE, the trade unions, professional and non-government organisations, business people and religious set up popular parliaments in different provinces as alternative authorities. In the Sierra province of Azuay, 500 km south of Quito, the popular parliament presided over by archbishop Luna Tobar, was set up on Sunday, with the participation of more than 50 delegations.

These parliaments discussed regional problems, and worked out proposals to present to a national parliament, which will be established this Tuesday in Quito. 'The objective is to present a political, economic and social plan,' and seek 'the best solution for the benefit of the country,' said indigenous leader Ricardo Ulcuango. He warned that the indigenous would not allow members of any political party to take part in the parliament.

The protests, the setting up of the peoples' parliament and the demand that the three state powers should resign took place when the results became known of the poll conducted by the firm Cedatos, which appears to demonstrate the unpopularity of the democratic system. In a rating from 1 to 100, the people consulted by Cedatos gave more than 50 points to the family, the Catholic church, the armed forces, the universities, the social movements and the media. Below 15 points came democracy, the banks, the government, the judicial system, the national parliament and the political parties.

MAURICIO USHIÑA

'At the moment none of the functions of the state – executive, parliament and judiciary – have the people's confidence,' said Polivio Córdoba, director of Cedatos. Likewise, 92 per cent of those consulted by Cedatos consider that Mahuad should resign or change direction. Only 2 per cent said he should remain in power.

'When a clear majority calls for the resignation of the president, Dr Mahuad should listen carefully to the reasons for this rare unanimity in a republic which is not exactly characterised by the ease with which it reaches great agreement,' said Franciso Huerta Montalvo, deputy-director of the daily paper *Expreso*.

If Mahuad 'listens well and is honest with himself, he will understand that he is the one who is wrong and not the people,' said Huerta Montalvo, who took part in the economy committee of the people's parliament and came out totally against dollarisation because it would involve enormous social costs.

Defence minister general José Gallardo declared that the armed forces would keep order and that the

indigenous uprising 'is one of the most dramatic phenomena to have occurred in the last few years' in Ecuador.

Luna Tobar asked the military and police not to repress the indigenous uprising because the government was threatening to repress any popular mobilisation and impose a state of emergency. 'It is clear that we are in an emergency, but I am confident that the public forces will be able to manage the situation and will not repress by force people who are unhappy with the bad situation in the country,' added Luna Tobar.

Vargas said the indigenous uprising would be national and indefinite. It will be intensified next Saturday with the take-over of public buildings, towns and banks. He asked representatives of international organisations in the country to watch the government in the next few days to prevent mass repression of the indigenous movement.

In the people's parliament, together with representatives of the indigenous communities, there were health workers' leaders, representatives of women's' organisations, human rights organisations, small business people, university lecturers, pensioners and peasants.

The former president of the supreme court, Carlos Solórzano Constantine, who was given the task of drawing up the legal bases of the alternative parliament, said: 'This popular assembly is legally based on article 1 of the constitution, which states that sovereignty rests with the people.'

Luna Tobar said the purpose of this parallel parliament is to announce that 'there is a free and sovereign people who wish to speak'. As for the opinion of the Ecuador Bishops' Conference that as a Catholic priest he cannot take part in politics, he indicated that he had not heard 'that canon law prohibited involvement in a meeting like this'.

Meanwhile, ex-president of the Central Bank, Pablo Better, who resigned because he did not agree with the dollarisation of the economy proposed by president Mahuad, said the government had changed its decision without taking into account the currency-issuing institution which 'has the prerogative of formulating exchange policy'.

Food prices have tripled in the past three days as a result of the announcement of the dollarisation. People flocked to the markets, fearing that food would become scarce with the indigenous protests. In some cities such as Cuenca there is already a shortage of supplies. In Guayaquil the transport strike continues which began on Monday because of the arrest of four trades union leaders and the clearing of streets by police and military. Small businesses are keeping their premises shut to take part in the Guayas people's parliament. This Tuesday social security workers took over the premises of the Ecuadorian Institute of Social Security and began an indefinite strike. The hospitals are also paralysed.

14 January 2000 (Thursday) A restricted document from the Central Bank of Ecuador warns that dollarisation could cause economic chaos. Meanwhile, the indigenous are hastening to mobilise 2 million people against the measure.

The study, presented to the government in December, indicates that conditions are not ripe to implement the dollarisation programme.

Experts say that in order to adopt dollarisation it is necessary to re-finance the state's liabilities and have a strong financial system to confront the massive withdrawal of deposits; otherwise, depositors would have no backing from the Central Bank. They also say monetary reserves would be too low to buy all the *sucres* in circulation, as the dollarisation plan proposes.

A technical expert from the Central Bank, who asked to remain anonymous, told Inter Press Service that without sufficient monetary reserves, 'we run the risk of running a dollarised economy for some sectors and a sucre economy for others, which would cause chaos'.

The restricted document also indicates that dollarisation limits the potential for using monetary policy to deal with possible world financial crises or devaluations in neighbouring countries, which would reduce the competitiveness of Ecuadorian products.

The same technical expert explained that Ecuador's economic situation is very different from that of Argentina when it adopted convertibility. 'Argentina is a much more powerful economy. Ecuador has not even been able to consolidate a capitalist economy in many indigenous and peasant sectors, which will not be able to go over to the dollar and perhaps will revert to barter,' he said.

According to this expert, if in a relatively powerful economy like Argentina 'unemployment rose from 6 per cent to 18 per cent with convertibility, which is not an irreversible policy, in Ecuador the effects would be much more negative'. Unemployment in Ecuador is 18.1 per cent and under-employment, 'which in this country is almost the same thing,' is 54.4. per cent, and if these two indicators increase, 'there will be social chaos,' he said.

Mahuad's government knew about the Central Bank's report and knows that the country is not ready for dollarisation, the expert added. 'Nevertheless, it changed its attitude from one moment to the next, perhaps to overcome its own instability, by gaining the support of certain political and business sectors in favour of the measure.'

The minister of human development, Juan Falconí, and other government spokesmen, said dollarisation was decided on after a detailed study of its feasibility and consequences, and that monetary reserves were sufficient. As for the Central Bank document, it merely expresses one of the points of view manifested in the discussion before the announcement of dollarisation.

The document points out the need for an integral economic programme in the short term, and suggests that the government has never had one. It also indicates that dollarisation is an extreme fixed-exchange type of scheme, which had been much discussed in academic circles, just as at the time there was much discussion of flotation and exchange bands, 'but up till now the proposal is still basically at the experimental stage'.

It also explains that the academic discussion indicated as advantages the reduction of inflation and interest rates, which would create an atmosphere of confidence for investment.

The source consulted by Inter Press Service observed that dollarisation or convertibility do not of themselves cause a recovery of confidence in an economy, although they can make for price stability, as happened in Argentina. Some Argentine businessmen 'prefer to invest their profits in foreign banks, like the US$7 billion they hold in Uruguay, instead of keeping them in institutions in their own country or investing them in production. This means that

industries are closing down and unemployment is increasing,' said the source.

The indigenous and social movements decided to respond to dollarisation with an indefinite national protest, demanding the removal of the three state powers. CONAIE began to block roads and prevent the entry of agricultural products into the cities. Beginning on Saturday it plans to mobilise nearly 2 million people.

This week various cities woke up to find the military had moved in and public buildings were guarded by soldiers and police, to prevent them being occupied by demonstrators. About 25,000 troops have been mobilised to respond to the protest, but the defence minister and chief of the joint command of the armed forces, general Carlos Mendoza, promised CONAIE that they would not repress the uprising if it proceeded peacefully. Mendoza took over as defence minister on Wednesday after general José Gallardo had resigned because he did not have the support of the armed forces.

Some 300 peasants have detained 20 officials in the city of Tulcán, on the frontier with Colombia. Among these were the governor of the province of Carchi, several mayors, the managing director of the National Promotion Bank and a woman member of parliament. Transport continues to be paralysed in the city of Guayaquil.

Mahuad asked the population to accept dollarisation as the only solution to avoid hyperinflation. Nevertheless, the new monetary conversion scheme has caused the price of products in the market to rise between 50 and 300 per cent in barely five days, while the majority of the population refuses to use the dollar as a currency.

MAURICIO USHIÑA

Women of the Otavalo nation, from Imbabura, walking to Quito, January 2000.

Journey to the rainbow

15 January 2000 (Saturday) The indigenous movement and other social sectors began their indefinite uprising to demand the removal of the three state powers. The country is expected to be completely paralysed.

The protests, which had been announced for next Saturday, were brought forward in response to president Jamil Mahuad's decision to dollarise the economy and to privatise public assets to combat a deep economic crisis.

The decision to dollarise shows that the government is listening only to bankers and big agro-exporters, who are demanding this measure, says CONAIE.

Indigenous leaders announced that the national protest would not end until Mahuad resigns, parliament is dissolved and members of the supreme court are removed. They also declared that they would not accept a simple exchange of national authorities. They demanded the installation of a new 'government concerned with the interests of the people', with participation by the armed forces, social groups and independent professionals.

'It is possible that many Ecuadorians are not in agreement with the indigenous demand to reduce the three state powers to zero and reconstitute power from its base upwards,' said political analyst Javier Ponce. 'It is possible that [this proposal] has no viability, since it involves a constitutional breakdown and the imminent danger of a military dictatorship. But it has the merit of demanding change beyond the simple removal of Mahuad.'

The indigenous 'are not talking of taking power for themselves. Accusing them of this and mocking the supposed pretensions of Miguel Lluco or Nina Pacari is an infantile manoeuvre by the interior minister Vladimiro Alvarez Grau, that smacks of desperation,' said Ponce. 'Few people understand that the indigenous movement starts from a discourse that may sound radical but is out to achieve what is possible,' he said.

Mahuad intends to shore up his government by a pact with the Ecuadorian Roldosista Party of ex-president Abdalá Bucaram, the support of the United States and the armed forces, although there are differing opinions among the military.

'the indigenous movement starts from a discourse that may sound radical but is out to achieve what is possible'

The pact with the Roldosistas is designed to consolidate a parliamentary majority to prevent parliament sacking Mahuad. In exchange, the government will allow Bucaram to return to Ecuador, from where he had been banned.

The president also intends to secure Washington's support. In this respect, chancellor Benjamín Ortíz stated that Bill Clinton's government will negotiate resources for Ecuador from the IMF. However, few Ecuadorians believe the chancellor's statement.

Likewise, the authorities are not ignoring the military, although it is said that some officers sympathise with the indigenous proposals and some have withdrawn their support for former defence minister, retired general José Gallardo, forcing him to resign.

Nevertheless, the Extended Council of Generals and Admirals of the Armed Forces issued a communiqué expressing their decision to 'reject any intention of breaking with the legal order'. However, for some analysts this message was directed at Mahuad and some of his ministers, who had

proposed to general Carlos Mendoza that he should support a government coup. This same council demanded 'that the powers of the state, the political parties and society in general should solve the crisis within the constitutional and democratic framework.'

17 January (Monday) The president of CONAIE, Antonio Vargas, has denounced the arrest of three trades union leaders and announced that between Tuesday and Wednesday a march of thousands of indigenous would arrive in Quito.

Ciro Guzmán, national president of the Popular Democratic Movement, Luis Villacís of the Patriotic Front and José Chaves of the United Workers' Front were arrested last Saturday in the Guzmán's house by a group of hooded men, who surrounded the building and broke doors and windows. Vargas said: 'Because the government is no longer a government, it is beginning to repress.'

Ecuador is in a state of emergency, with all guarantees of individual rights suspended. Since it was declared 10 days ago, more than 40 people have been arrested. Interior minister, Vladimiro Alvarez, was summoned before the Parliamentary Investigation Committee to explain the forced entry into the home of the trades union leaders, as well as reports of ill-treatment of citizens arrested during the protest.

Cities and roads across the country remained militarised to prevent the indigenous taking over roads and public offices. The armed forces have been given orders to prevent the advance of thousands of indigenous towards Quito, which has delayed the march on the capital.

In the northern provinces, all indigenous travelling in commercial buses towards the capital have been told to get out and continue their journey on foot. This represents a form of apartheid against the Indians and highlights the country's latent racism.

As part of the protest, this Monday the indigenous maintained some roadblocks in the south-eastern province of Morona Santiago, in Amazonia, on the frontier with Peru. The roads in the southern Sierra provinces of Cañar, Azuay and Loja, are blocked as are some stretches of road in Chimborazo in the central Sierra, and the northern provinces of Imbabura and Carchi.

On Sunday about 3,000 people took part in a march called by the indigenous and social movements in the city of Ibarram, capital of Imbabura. In Cuenca, several thousand women staged an empty saucepan march[27], which was introduced by the church bells ringing. There were also protest marches in several mid-Sierra cities and markets for farm products closed in many provinces for fear of looting.

Vargas said the blockades would increase until roads were totally cut off. This has led to the fear of a shortage of supplies in food markets. The 6,500 workers in the state oil company, Petroecuador, joined the indigenous uprising on Monday, threatening a fuel shortage in the next few days. The oil workers threatened to cease producing oil in the five state oil fields, not to pump other companies' crude oil from Amazonia to the Esmeraldas refineries, situated on the country's northern Pacific coast, and not to load oil for export. The oil workers are opposed to dollarisation, which also involves privatisation of the hydro-carbons sector.

The president of the National Federation of Oil Workers of Ecuador

MAURICIO USHIÑA

Soldiers force passengers off buses and lorries on the way to Quito, January 2000.

(Fetrapec), Enrique Barros, said that during the strike, the state will cease to produce 210,000 barrels of oil, to pump 320,000 barrels and export 280,000 of crude oil per day. Barros did not rule out the possibility that oil workers might join in the takeover of oil wells by indigenous communities in the east of the country. Barros said that through dollarisation and the accompanying laws, 'the government is planning to surrender its main source of wealth [oil] to private enterprise. Last year alone oil contributed US$1.375 billion to the state budget.'

Meanwhile, the journal *Lideres* has

[27] A demonstration led by women heads of households who carry empty saucepans and beat them as a way of showing that, because of the economic situation, they do not have the money to buy food to fill them.

published a confidential World Bank report, according to which during 1999 social indicators of poverty in Ecuador deteriorated alarmingly, and the same tendency is continuing this year. According to the study, Ecuador has 5.1 million poor people and 1.9 million living in conditions of extreme poverty. It also states that to reduce inequality it is necessary significantly to improve access by poor sectors to basic health and education provision.

18 January 2000 (Tuesday) President Jamil Mahuad today consulted technical experts in the foundation directed by Argentina's former economy minister, Domingo Cavallo, to make the final adjustments to the laws on dollarisation of the economy. At the meeting were Guillermo Mondino and Jorge Vasconcelos, of the Mediterranean Foundation, José Luis Moreno of the Bank of Panama, and Eugenio Pendaz and Pablo Guidotti, ex-superintendent of banks and former vice-minister of finance in Argentina respectively.

They spent several hours analysing the economic effects of dollarisation, together with ministers, technical experts from the Central Bank and Ecuador's superintendent of banks.

Meanwhile, the protests against dollarisation are continuing with road blocks and marches in different parts of the country. On Tuesday morning more than 8,000 indigenous arrived in Quito to take part in the symbolic takeover of the city. A further 10,000 are expected.

The authorities analysed the disposable monetary reserves to buy up all the *sucres* in circulation and free the bank deposits frozen by the government last March. They did not report on their conclusions. The banks can return the money belonging to those who hold deposits of less than US$4,000, while those who have more than this must wait between seven and 10 years. Where banks collapsed and were taken over by the state, the payout will be in the form of official 10-year bonds tradeable on the stock exchange. According to experts, this will involve a loss to savers, as the bonds will be set at a much lower value than their savings.

Mahuad had opposed convertibility when it was proposed by Abdalá Bucaram, and as mayor of Quito had contributed to his sacking in 1997. Some analysts consider that the fact that foreign technical experts are only now being consulted over the dollarisation laws shows that the government has adopted the measure without proper planning. Businessman Andrés Vallejo, government minister during the presidency of Rodrigo Borja (1988-92), said Mahuad had adopted dollarisation 'as a way of combating the demand for his resignation, which was becoming general'. He said it was regarded as a leap in the dark when it was analysed by government technical experts.

The managing director of the IMF, Michel Camdessus, denied on Monday the report by Ecuadorian government spokesmen that the IMF had announced its support for the measure. 'To be frank, dollarisation is not the kind of monetary policy that we would have recommended to Ecuador at this stage,' said Camdessus, during a recess in the meeting of African heads of state with the IMF in Gabon. He showed surprise at the measure because IMF technical experts had been talking to the Ecuadorian economic authorities to reach a new contingency agreement and 'the possibility of dollarisation was never mentioned'.

Meanwhile, in its 15 January issue, the *The Economist* said dollarisation in Ecuador is a 'move in a desperate political game'. 'Driven by panic, the proposal was poorly planned and ineptly explained,' said the English weekly. 'Next day, investors were still wondering what exactly Mr Mahuad meant by dollarisation.' *The Economist* warns that there is a risk that hyperinflation might cause total chaos in the financial system if dollarisation does not work.

To deal with its small monetary reserves and to sustain the dollarisation scheme in the face of possible foreign shocks, the government decided to put through an advance sale of US$300 million worth of oil and thus obtain resources in two weeks' times.

Members of parliament belonging to the ruling party manoeuvred with other political forces to gain the necessary votes to put through the dollarisation laws when the president introduced the bill to parliament. The government could count on the support of Abdalá Bucaram's

Roldosista Party, whose technical experts are collaborating in the preparatory stage for dollarisation. They hope that the right-wing Social Christian Party will also vote in favour of dollarisation. But there are still some doubts because last week members of parliament belonging to the PSC did not contribute the majority necessary to name the directors of the Central Bank, who will be in charge of implementing dollarisation. The directors had to be nominated by decree.

19 January 2000 (Wednesday)

Ecuador is semi-paralysed by protests and road blocks, while 12,000 indigenous remain in Quito to prevent the approval of dollarisation proposed by president Jamil Mahuad. The indigenous are demanding the removal of the three state powers – the executive, the legislature and the judiciary.

The armed forces mobilised 25,000 troops to control the roads and prevent the passage of any private of commercial vehicle containing indigenous. This was denounced by human rights organisations as racist.

The indigenous evaded military control by mobilising in small groups, in canvas-covered lorries by secondary roads or by walking across country and mountains. In Quito they set up a camp in the Arbolito Park, three blocks from the national parliament. They were kept under close surveillance by the army. Some inhabitants and small traders of Quito came out in solidarity with the indigenous and brought them food.

According to Inter Press Service, on the access roads to the city the march towards the capital has not been stopped. Hundreds of indigenous men, women, old people and children continue to come, carrying bags of

'This uprising is like giving birth. It has just begun but when the *guagua* [baby in Quechua] is born they will see how strong it is.'

potatoes and vegetables to eat in the capital.

The indigenous were welcomed by the National Parliament of the Peoples of Ecuador, set up a week ago with 330 representatives of social movements, the indigenous, religious, humanitarian and non-government organisations, small business people, professionals and small traders.

Indigenous leader Blanca Chancoso says: 'This uprising is like giving birth. It has just begun but when the *guagua* [baby in Quechua] is born they will see how strong it is. It is already showing this by paralysing most of the country.'

The seat of the legislative parliament and the government palace are being guarded by the police and army. The surrounding streets are guarded by barbed wire and anti-riot vehicles. Uniformed men are posted on roof tops, armed with rifles with telescopic sights. Two helicopters are flying over the city keeping watch and dropping leaflets calling on the population not to join the protest.

'Our brothers and sisters have marched peacefully from different corners of the country, on foot or in lorries. Even though the armed forces are trying to delay their arrival, we know that in the next few days they will get here. It is a question of time,' said indigenous leader Miguel Lluco.

Various roads in the Sierra, the coast and Amazonia have been blocked with rocks and trees. And the demonstrators have dug trenches paralysing vehicle traffic. The southern provinces of Azuay, Cañar and Loja are cut off by land from the rest of the country. In the Amazon provinces of Napo, Morona, Santiago, Pastaza and Zamora Cinchipe the roads have been blocked and there have been many demonstrations. Meanwhile in Sucumbíos, on the frontier with Colombia, the inhabitants have surrounded the airport, stopping air traffic. The

MAURICIO USHIÑA

With main roads blocked, indigenous found alternative routes into the capital in January 2000.

Andean cities of Cuenca, Azoguez, Ibarra, Latacunga, Riobamba and Ambato are partially isolated by protests and road closures. Hundreds of peasants from the coastal provinces of Esmeraldas, Manabí, El Oro, Los Ríos and Guayas burned tyres on the roads and there were confrontations with police and soldiers who tried to clear them away.

Workers in Petroecuador have stopped pumping crude oil from Amazonia to the Esmeraldas refineries on the north coast. They are not loading crude oil for export and not distributing fuel. A shortage of supplies is expected.

In the capital and other cities there have been protest marches. The president of CONAIE, Antonio Vargas, said the protests will be progressive and over a long period. 'In a resistance struggle, you can't tell how long it will last, but we are prepared to carry on for as long as it takes,' Vargas told Inter Press Service.

Ecuador's former president Rodrigo Borja (1988-92) condemned the fact that the military are preventing the indigenous travelling to Quito, as a 'totally reprehensible racist measure'.

Alexis Ponce, spokesman of the Permanent Assembly for Human Rights, said that in the next few days, representatives of human rights organisations and European parliamentarians will be travelling to Ecuador to check whether the indigenous are being ill-treated and to check the prisons. Ponce said the state of emergency that has been in force in the country for the past two weeks, violates the rights laid down in the Ecuadorian constitution. There have been more than 100 arrests of leaders since the beginning of the protests.

Presidential spokesman Carlos Larreátegui said the government is prepared to talk with the indigenous if they relinquish their demand for the removal of the three state powers. 'We will not talk with CONAIE until it gives up this demand,' said Larreátegui, modifying the government's initial position that the mobilisation would have no impact at all. Development minister Juan Falconí met representatives of the chambers of commerce in an attempt to prevent the rise in prices, which has continued unabated since Mahuad announced the dollarisation of the economy on 5 January.

Businessmen declared that the price rises 'had been fair and were caused by increased costs,' so they would not take notice of any plea from the government. Falconí declared that the government would free up imports to combat the price rises. Business leaders opposed this. 'We are not afraid of threats, let them go ahead whenever they want,' stated Gustavo Pinto, president of the Chamber of Industry.

Stymied by the mobilisations and the 50 to 300 per cent increase in the price of basic goods over the past week, Mahuad hopes to be able to present the bills required to impose dollarisation of the economy to parliament this Friday.

Today the indigenous of Ecuador suggested to the military authorities the establishment of a 'government of national salvation', consisting of religious organisations, the armed forces and civil society.

Meanwhile, the protests against the government of Jamil Mahuad are intensifying. This Wednesday 15,000 people, including indigenous, peasants and residents of Quito marched to the ministry of defence. A group of leaders held a meeting with the minister and the chief of the joint command, Carlos Mendoza, to demand that the military should not repress the mobilisations and to take

RIDDLES IN THE PARK

19 January 2000

LORI WASELCHUK

After returning empty-handed from their talks at the defence ministry, the indigenous camping in El Arbolito Park are preparing their dinner. Among the large majority of Quechuas there is a Shuar who took part in the Cenepa war. 'This is another war,' he says and recalls one of his people's poems:

In the shiver of reiterated singing
there where the *tsunki* [spirits] float
there I am quivering
everything, nothing is difficult for me.
I am in the dream-zebra-singing
there where the songs are
I am where nothing is difficult
where the *supai* [gods] arise
I am there in the dream-zebra-singing.

Some indigenous from Cotopaxi are entertaining themselves by telling riddles. For the indige-

nous Quechua of the Andes, riddles are an important part of their lives. The riddles of the Andean indigenous can carry us on a humming bird's wings, take us to the moon, hypnotize us with a maize plant, let us hear the murmuring of the river descending the mountain and discover the mystery of the high snows. These riddles also recall the old traditions and, above all, the cosmic vision of the indigenous peoples.

When anyone asks how they were collected, they are told that in them 'you see, hear, touch, smell and taste the meaning our land has had for thousands of peasants and indigenous from antiquity right up to our days'. For Carlos David Kleymeyer (see Bibliography) the riddles of the Andes are short metaphorical poems. 'Normally,' he says, 'they are not jokes or word play, as in western culture, except for those that have been borrowed from that culture. When you hear an Ecuadorian Quechua or Peruvian-Bolivian Quechua riddle, there is a recognition between the one who asks and the one who answers. Instead of a sense of competition or joking between them, the Andean riddle is as if at daybreak one person opens the window to another,' says Kleymeyer.

I remember his saying now while I am standing outside the Casa de la Cultura, where a group of indigenous have met to tell each other riddles. Miguel asks the others: 'What is a sky without stars?' A few minutes pass and the correct answer is not forthcoming. Suddenly Luis says: 'The mirror,' to which Miguel nods his assent. Everyone asks Luis how he guessed it and he gives the following answer: 'It was very simple. I remembered that yesterday we had been talking about the difference between this sky full of buildings, in which we cannot see ourselves in spite of it being a mirror, and the Tigua sky full of stars.'

Imashi for the Ecuadorian Quechua, *watuchis* for the Peruvian Quechua, riddles are a mirror of their culture.

---

up a position towards the crisis the country is going through.

Ricardo Ulcuango, leader of CONAIE, said the indigenous asked Mendoza 'to keep his promise and not repress the peaceful protests and to declare whether military support would be for the corrupt men governing the country or for the people,' said Ulcuango.

They also gave Mendoza the plan for a popular government drawn up by the National Parliament of the Peoples of Ecuador. Mendoza said he understood the indigenous demands and the poverty in which they lived. However, he insisted that the armed forces would respect the institutional order. He also criticised the social movements, saying there were also corrupt people in their ranks. He questioned the dollarisation plan, announced by Mahuad last week to resolve the economic crisis facing the country.

Meanwhile, about 35,000 people from different social sectors marched into the centre of Cuenca, capital of the province of Azuay and the country's third city, 500 km from Quito. The archbishop of Cuenca, Luis

'The people are not asking for the breakdown of institutions. They are only asking that these should be in the service of the great majority, so that there might be true democracy,'

Alberto Luna Tobar, who led the march, said that this was 'only the beginning of the triumph', and that he considered the fact that the military did not permit the indigenous to travel to Quito 'an unprecedented act of violence and racism'.

'The people are not asking for the breakdown of institutions. They are only asking that these should be in the service of the great majority, so that there might be true democracy,' said the archbishop. Peasants and members of social movements have occupied the local government building of Azuay province.

Poncho utopia

20 January 2000 (Thursday) 10 am
About 12,000 indigenous have surrounded the parliament building and the supreme court in Quito, while soldiers and police armed with guns, machine guns and tear gas formed a ring to prevent the indigenous occupying these buildings.

Officials and members of parliament decided to leave the seat of the legislature, in case the indigenous managed to occupy it. Roads in the Sierra, the coast and Amazonia have been blocked by rocks and trees and the demonstrators dug trenches, paralysing vehicle traffic. The southern provinces of Azuay, Cañar and Loja are cut off by land from the rest of the country. In the Amazon provinces of Napo, Morona, Santiago and Zamora Chinchipe, the roads have been blocked, there have been numerous demonstrations and the markets are closed. In Sucumbíos, on the frontier with Colombia, local inhabitants have closed the airport to air traffic. In Napo 300 metres of the aqueduct carrying water to Tena, the provincial capital, have been destroyed. Most of the city districts have no water. The Andean cities of Cuenca, Azoguez, Ibarra, Latacunga, Riobamba and Ambato are partially isolated by protests and road blocks. There is beginning to be a shortage of farm products, gas and fuel. Hundreds of peasants from the coastal provinces of Esmeraldas, Manabí, El Oro, Los Ríos and Guayas set fire to tyres on the roads and confronted police and military trying to clear them away.

Workers in the state oil company (Petroecuador) are continuing to refuse to pump oil from Amazonia to the Esmeraldas refineries, on the north coast. They are also refusing to load crude oil for export or to distribute fuel. The shortage of supplies is now being felt.

The coastal city of Portoviejo, capital of the province of Mannabí, was symbolically taken over by 4,000 peasants from different areas, and various towns in the Sierra were taken over by farm workers. Ibarra, two hours away from Quito, was also taken over this Thursday by 5,000 indigenous, who arrived from different communities to protest outside the town hall.

Leader of the National Peasant Co-ordinating Committee, Rosa Criollo, said peasants from all over the country will remain mobilised indefinitely, together with the indigenous. 'As well as blocking roads, we will continue occupying government houses and towns throughout the country,' declared Criollo.

Trades unionists from the National Electricity Company have joined the protests, and their leaders did not rule out the possibility that in the next few hours they will cut off the power in certain areas of the country.

Five days after the beginning of the indigenous and popular uprising, there have been more than 200 arrests and more than 20 demonstrators have been wounded by police.

Although the interior minister Vladimiro Alvarez stated that the protests lacked strength, officials indicated to the press the possibility of talks with the indigenous to seek a solution to the crisis.

However, Jorge Loor, one of the leaders of the uprising, declared that the only solution is the establishment of a government of national consensus. 'This government must emphasise the country's monetary

LORI WASELCHUK

MAURICIO USHIÑA

People from shanty-towns around Quito came out in support of the indigenous protests in January 2000.

sovereignty and reject dollarisation,' he said.

Loor also declared that it is necessary to 'encourage the productive sector, modernise state companies so that they can be efficient without being privatised, reduce foreign debt payment, create an emergency social fund against poverty and to imprison the bankers who plundered the country'.

21 January 2000 (Friday) 10am The military ring surrounding the parliament collapses. After the initial confusion everyone runs inside the building. There are no longer any tear gas bombs, barbed wire or guns to hold back this march. Some look astonished. Among the threadbare ponchos walks a group of army officers who have decided to support the demonstrators. More than 2,000 indigenous, supported by the military,

occupy the parliament. They refuse to recognise the government, and appoint a Junta of National Salvation. For many this all sounds like utopia, but utopia also needs a little help.

The junta consists of colonel Lucio Gutiérrez, the indigenous leader Antonio Vargas, and ex-president of the supreme court, Carlos Solórzano. Gutiérrez declares that it is a revolution against corruption and poverty. He asks the international community to recognise 'the sovereignty' of the Ecuadorian people. 'This is no overnight subversive movement. It has been carefully thought out and planned and we the military are on the side of the indigenous,' says Gutiérrez.

He states that the role of the armed forces is to defend national sovereignty and support the people in their most heartfelt demands, their suffering. 'It is not the task of the military to defend a government of corrupt bankers with the excuse of maintaining an institutional order that is violated every day by those in government,' says Gutiérrez.

The National Parliament of the Peoples of Ecuador was also established in the national parliament building, with the participation of indigenous, peasants, representatives of social movements and non-governmental organisations, independent professionals and small business people.

The junta issued its first decrees seeking restriction orders on Mahuad, the president of the parliament, Juan José Pons, and the president of the supreme court, Galo Pico. The restriction order prevents them from leaving the country.

Meanwhile, colonel Gutiérrez declared that this was a peaceful movement, fighting to restore the self-esteem and dignity of the people of Ecuador. 'People, arise and fight to eliminate the corruption and impunity sponsored by this government. Arise to say no to the robbery of the millennium, instigated by the banks,' said Gutiérrez.

He also called for unity to 'restore democracy with generosity,' and thus 'carry the country forward'. The colonel exhorted 'ex-presidents, honest politicians, the media and all the women and men who love this country' to support the junta. 'This is an historic moment. We must unite, because if we don't, the country will disintegrate,' he warned.

The president of the parliament, Pons, called on the members of parliament to attend an extraordinary meeting this Saturday in the Central Bank building in the city of Guayaquil. But members of parliament for the Pachakutik Movement and the Democratic Left recognised the junta

and offered their resignations 'in the service of the people'.

General Paco Moncayo, who was chief of the joint command of the Ecuadorian armed forces during the border war between Ecuador and Peru in 1995, said the uprising had been predictable. 'When those in charge do not eliminate the corruption suffered by this country with this government, officers come forward to seek solutions, as happened in Venezuela, when Hugo Chaves [the current president] rose up,' said Moncayo. 'There is nothing different in the case of Ecuador [from that of Venezuela]. An even moderately sensitive president would have had to resign by now,' he added.

Colonel Gutiérrez, who took an active part in the war against Peru, was compared to Chaves by a military source, for 'his Bolivarian talk and his links with the poorest sectors of society'. He had already sparked an incident within the armed forces by demanding that the authorities should take sides 'against the corruption being shown in the bank collapses and their bailing out by the government'.

The president of CONAIE, Antonio Vargas, one of the leaders in the takeover of parliament, said that events today are a result of the government's 'insensitivity'. 'This uprising of the Ecuadorian people has been completely peaceful, and it is being recognised in every corner of the country where people are continuing to rise up, taking over government houses and protesting against the system that has prevailed until today,' declared Vargas. Utopia is gathering strength.

BLOOD, FROGS AND BIOPIRACY
21 January 2000

A shaman blesses the takeover of parliament, he scares off the evil spirits, and drinks a *ayahuasca*[28] toast to it. At the end of the ceremony, he recalls in a trance the time a few months back when five shamans from the Amazon region went to the United States to ask that country's government to revoke the patent on the use of *ayahuasca*.

In November 1999 the US Patent Office was forced to recognise its error and annul the patent on this sacred plant. *Ayahuasca*, which can produce hallucinogenic effects, is considered sacred by the natives of Amazonia and they attribute curative properties to it. Amazonia includes territories belonging to Bolivia, Brazil, Colombia, Ecuador, French Guayana, Guyana, Peru, Venezuela and Suriname.

'Sacred plants used in collective cultural practices cannot be patented, because their commercialisation offends indigenous peoples,' the shamans maintain. The case of *ayahuasca* is one of countless other cases of 'biopiracy' (appropriation of biological resources) of the natural wealth of Amazonia.

In Ecuador, whose biological diversity relative to its size is the greatest in Latin America, there has been an outcry about the use of natural resources for genetic investigation by many foreign companies.

Spokespersons for the conservationist organisation Ecological Action say various foreign companies are organising research programmes employing anthropologists and ethno-biologists to obtain genetic resources in Amazonia. One example is the Petrolera Maxus company, which

set up the Yasun' scientific station a few months ago in Ecuadorian Amazonia. According to the agreement signed with Ecuador, Maxus is bound to pass on its technology to Ecuador and share part of the profits with the Ecuadorian state and the indigenous communities who are the custodians of biodiversity. But Maxus is failing to honour this commitment. International scientific reviews have denounced the fact that biological resources extracted by Maxus are used in the pharmaceutical industry.

Two years ago, 750 live frogs were taken out of Ecuador. Their skin was used to produce an analgesic 200 times stronger than morphine. This was done without any benefit whatsoever to Ecuador. This analgesic was patented in the United States by the company Shaman Pharmaceuticals, which according to a report in the *Wall Street Journal*, was founded in 1989 on the basis that 'the knowledge of the shamans about medicinal plants could help us find curative compounds and make profits from them'.

Something similar occurred with *quinua*, a plant from the Andean region. They isolated the genes in it that makes it rich in proteins, in order to incorporate them into other plants.

The Awa indigenous community, who inhabit the northern coast of Ecuador and some areas of Colombia, collaborated with the US National Cancer Institute in collecting and investigating plants which could be used in the production of medicines against AIDS and cancer.

Beyond the importance of these investigations, the Ecuadorian indigenous are wondering what benefits they will obtain for themselves and for Ecuador when they hand over their biological resources.

According to the Agreement on Biodiversity signed at the UN Conference on Environment

---

[28] *Ayahuasca*: South American narcotic plant, from which a drink inducing delirium and hallucinations is obtained (Latin: *bannisteria mettalicolor*).

and Development, held in Rio de Janeiro in 1992,[29] biological resources are part of national sovereignty. This means that both the state and the indigenous communities must know the results of investigations employing their biological resources and obtain benefits from them. Yet frequently this does not happen. The same agreement establishes that scientific investigation must aim to conserve biological diversity and promote its sustainable use.

The Carthage Agreement, created by the Andean Pact, requires that when member countries (Bolivia, Colombia, Ecuador, Peru and Venezuela) sign contracts with companies investigating genetic resources, the indigenous communities affected must be previously consulted.

Last year indigenous representatives from Colombia and Ecuador began a joint legal action

[29] The United States has not signed.

to recover blood samples taken to the United States. At the same time they pushed for the approval of laws protecting biodiversity in their respective countries.

The indigenous leader Ricardo Ulcuango says research into the blood of indigenous communities was an attack on Ecuadorian biodiversity, but also infringes the human rights of these communities. 'We knew about the stealing of sacred animals and plants like *ayahuasca* but it had not yet reached the point of actually carrying off our brothers' and sisters' blood.' he added.

According to the French microbiologist Albert Sasson, from the University of Paris, research in biotechnology tends to satisfy the needs of international markets and not those of developing countries. 'Thus we are running the risk of widening the technological breach between the rich and poor countries even more. We must define a strategy to distribute the benefits of biotechnology fairly,' he declared.

21 January 2000 (Friday) 4pm The armed forces of Ecuador demand the resignation of president Jamil Mahuad. But he challenges his opponents to take power by force, after insisting he will not resign.

'We have asked the president to resign for the good of the country, to prevent a social explosion,' general Carlos Mendoza, chief of the joint command, stated publicly, Mendoza declared that the military was 'monolithically' united and exhorted the government to be 'sensitive' to the situation of economic crisis and with the mobilisation of popular forces demanding the resignation of the three powers of the state.

Mahuad declared on network radio and television that what was happening was an attempted coup with the object of imposing a dictatorship and that he would not accept his own removal. 'If this is going to be a military coup to take power by force, ladies and gentlemen, well, let them take power by force,' said the president to confirm his

determination to stay in government.

Former president Rodrigo Borja said there was no constitutional solution and that Mahuad 'must go to avoid confrontations between the people'.

21 January 2000 6pm The chiefs of Ecuador's armed forces establish themselves in the government house, after the departure of president Mahuad in the direction of the air base. The military chiefs await the arrival of the leaders of the popular uprising to negotiate a solution to the constitutional crisis.

Vice-president Gustavo Noboa arrived in Quito from Guayaquil on the coast, backed by political leaders who are invoking constitutional legality to promote him as the new president.

Before abandoning the seat of executive power, Mahuad broadcast a message on network television and radio that he would not resign, despite the strength of the civil-

'If this is going to be a military coup to take power by force, ladies and gentlemen, well, let them take power by force,' said the president

military movement demanding his replacement by a Junta of National Salvation and pressure from the armed forces for his resignation.

The indigenous leader Antonio Vargas, one of the three members of the junta, said Mahuad's government was now actually at an end. Vargas announced that the junta, consisting of himself, colonel Lucio Gutiérrez and the ex-president of the supreme court Carlos Solórzano, would take over the presidency.

The Junta of National Salvation asked the military joint command, headed by the acting minister of defence, general Carlos Mendoza, to recognise it as the legitimate authority. A few hours earlier, Mendoza had publicly reported that the joint command of the armed forces had demanded Mahuad's resignation 'to avoid a social explosion'.

Officers of other military

detachments from the province of Azuay and other regions refused to obey their superiors and pledged themselves to the junta. In Guayaquil the navy awaits the outcome of events.

In Washington, the Organisation of American States (OAS) declared an emergency session. The OAS secretary-general, César Gaviria, who was in Paris, declared his 'strong condemnation of this act [the uprising in Ecuador] contrary to democratic principles currently operating in the hemisphere'.

The Rio Group also expressed concern about 'the events developing in Ecuador' and its 'strong rejection of any attempt to upset the constitutional order and democratic institutions of that country'.

The US government exhorted all parties to respect constitutional order, said White House spokesman, Mike Hammer. The 15 member countries of the European Union asked for respect for institutional legality in Ecuador, and Spain's foreign minister considered that the occupation of the parliament building by the indigenous and their military allies was especially 'serious'. The US embassy began to press for the vice-president Gustavo Noboa to take over.

21 January 2000, 8pm The leaders of the civil-military uprising have entered the government house to negotiate with the joint command of the armed forces over a solution to the constitutional crisis.

The Junta of National Salvation, appointed by indigenous, peasants, social leaders and officers who had distanced themselves from the chain of military command, refuses to recognise the three powers of the state and claims itself to be the only legitimate authority, said Antonio Vargas, leader of CONAIE.

Vargas and the other members of the junta, colonel Lucio Gutiérrez, and Carlos Solórzano arrived at the Carondelet palace accompanied by thousands of demonstrators. The members of the junta held talks in the seat of government with general Carlos Mendoza, chief of the joint command of the armed forces, and with other officers. The military are divided over the crisis, even though Mendoza is maintaining control of the majority of units.

Miguel Lluco, of CONAIE, declared that Jamil Mahuad's government was irreversibly dissolved. Despite having said that he would not resign, Mahuad abandoned the government house after his government was disowned by the joint command of the armed forces. He made for the air force base in Quito, apparently planning to travel to Chile. According to some versions, officers at the air base prevented him from leaving the country, in accordance with the junta's first decree, which prohibited him from travelling abroad.

Vice-president Gustavo Noboa has arrived in Quito from Guayaquil, supported by political leaders who want him to be the next president.

The military top brass had prepared a proclamation telling the country of their intention to declare themselves dictators. The leaders of CONAIE and the colonels do not agree with this. Everyone is speaking about avoiding confrontations, which could lead to deaths. The insurgents are supported by part of the army, the indigenous movement and the social organisations, which are continuing the streets protests, taking over government and public buildings in various provinces.

The television channels are intensifying their campaign against the popular government, begun during the afternoon with a succession of politicians and businessmen calling for a coup to make Gustavo Noboa president, so that dollarisation can continue. Many are packing their bags, because they fear that if the junta consolidates its power, it will send them to prison on grounds of corruption. In what appears to have been an order given by a high official, all television channels just happened to give their telephone numbers so that officers who did not agree with the uprising led by the colonels and the indigenous could phone in. As Mahuad still refuses to resign, the pro-Noboa conspiracy begins to gather strength.

MAURICIO USHIÑA

People in Quito's Plaza de Independencia, celebrating the taking of the presidential palace and the formation of the popular government, 21 January 2000.

The vice-president enters by the back door

22 January 2000 (Saturday) 1am The military authorities reach an agreement with the insurgents, by which a government junta is set up composed of general Carlos Mendoza, Carlos Solórzano and Antonio Vargas. Everyone in the government house puts their hands together and prays an 'Our Father' as a form of oath. Mendoza undertakes to respect the popular uprising and to attack corruption. He promises there will be no retaliation against rebel officers.

In the name of the top military command, general Telmo Sandoval continues talks with Gustavo Noboa and one of his close friends, to explain to him that events are developing in his favour, that soon he will be installed in Carondelet.

At 4am Mendoza receives a telephone call and leaves the government house for an hour and a half. When he returns he announces to the other two members of the triumvirate that he is resigning from the junta because his family has asked him to. He offers his hand to those who are present and no one will shake it, then he leaves. Shortly afterwards the other military begin to abandon Carondelet. Minutes later Antonio Vargas receives a call from general Telmo Sandoval to come to the joint command of the armed forces. The president of CONAIE, accompanied among others by indigenous leaders

Miguel Lluco, Luis Macas, Ricardo Ulcuango and Salvador Quishpe, arrives at the command, where Mendoza informs them that he has retired and tells them that vice-president Gustavo Noboa is assuming the presidency.

This declaration receives the support of the other top brass of the armed forces, thus beginning the process to stop the establishment in Ecuador of a civil-military government backed by the popular sectors.

The indigenous leaders denounce Mendoza but the game is up. 'Mendoza betrayed the indigenous and popular movement, and placed himself at the service of the corrupt men ruling this country,' said Vargas. 'After committing himself to respect the will of a people in the streets calling for an end to corrupt bankers and the same old politicians, Mendoza retreated, besmirching his military uniform. But we indigenous will remain mobilised and we will continue to be vigilant,' he added.

A few hours later colonel Gutiérrez is arrested by plain clothes men, who say they belong to army intelligence. The officer's wife, Ximena Bohorquez, tells the media that she fears for his life.

Noboa, who takes over the presidency this morning, at the headquarters of the armed forces, has the support of Jamil Mahuad, who returns to make clear that he did not resign because 'an overthrown president has not resigned or abandoned his office'.

Mahuad's refusal to resign makes it necessary for parliament to pass a motion stating that he had abandoned his office. This takes place at noon today in Guayaquil at an extraordinary session. The right-wing parties found the precise article of the constitution to support Noboa and justify the re-establishment of an institutional government, in which nobody in the country believes. 'Because Mahuad would not resign, technically there was a coup which left the office vacant and made the vice-president become president,' said a lawyer, who points out the similarity to the solution with 'what happened when parliament sacked Abdalá Bucaram, in February 1997, on the grounds that he was mentally unfit to govern'.

The only ones to vote against the measure were a few members of parliament belonging to the social democrat Democratic Left party. The Pachakutik Movement members did not attend the meeting.

In the morning, the indigenous and representatives of social organisations vacated the parliament building, which they had occupied since Friday, but they declared that the uprising and the peoples' parliament would carry on.

At the beginning, a few officers refused to recognise the nomination of Noboa 'for being part of Mahuad's government', but gradually the different military units were coming into line with the joint command of the armed forces.

Events of the past 24 hours have shown a rupture between the younger officers and the high military command, and above all the power of the Ecuadorian indigenous people to mobilise. The attempt to establish in Ecuador a popular government made up of military, indigenous and representatives of civil society was abortive, but a poll by the firm Cedatos confirmed that 71 per cent of the population supports the indigenous movement and 64 per cent backed the civil-military uprising.

22 January 2000, 8pm General Carlos Mendoza, ex-chief of the joint command of the armed forces and former defence minister of Ecuador, declared today that ex-president Jamil Mahuad intended to mount a coup similar to that of Alberto Fujimori in Peru. Before proposing the dollarisation of the Ecuadorian economy, two weeks ago, Mahuad suggested the dissolution of parliament to the military top brass, declared Mendoza.

'I did not accept this balderdash that he [Mahuad] was suggesting to us, to break with constitutional order, and I offered my resignation. But he did not have the courage to accept it and continue with his plan,' he declared.

Mendoza's statement came at the same time as Mahuad accused the military of having planned a coup to overthrow him.

Some analysts attributed Mendoza's subsequent resignation to international pressure, and in particular from the US embassy, which was unhappy with a government made up of military and indigenous.

Mendoza's statements cast doubt on Mahuad's democratic credentials, although he claimed always to have defended democracy. Meanwhile, the ex-president's accusations put a question mark over the new Ecuadorian government, which came about in an illegal manner. Furthermore, they raised the possibility that the military top brass had used the popular insurrection and afterwards disowned it, in order to carry out a coup to place Noboa in the presidency.

23 January 2000 (Sunday) The principal indigenous organisation of Ecuador, whose leaders have remained in hiding since the end of the insurrection on Friday, have rejected the new government's first decisions, which confirmed the dollarisation plan and announced a tough economic package. The president of CONAIE, Antonio Vargas, declared that the indigenous uprising had not been a failure because it had confirmed their organisational strength and power of mobilisation. 'We have shown that we are a force. We have learnt various lessons from this insurrection, so that we will not make the same mistakes again of believing in traitors like the military top brass,' he declared.

Vargas said the indigenous and social movements disagree with the outcome of the insurrection that they instigated on Friday, together with more than 100 army officers. 'We do not accept their making Mr Noboa president. He was Mahuad's vice-president and he took office without Mahuad resigning. We are watching what he does very carefully,' he said.

Vargas believes the signs are negative. He points to the fact that Noboa is ratifying dollarisation of the economy, announcing a tough structural adjustment package and supporting the superintendant of banks, who promoted the rise in the dollar, permitting speculation by banks managed by the state. Vargas referred to a denunciation by the Democratic Left member of parliament Carlos González, according to which the banks taken over by the state speculated with hundreds of millions of dollars in the last week of December and the first week of January, while the superintendant of banks remained impassive. 'That speculation made the dollar rise disproportionately, and the rise was the excuse to dollarise the country, a proposal with which we disagree, because it will only bring more hunger to the poor sectors,' said Vargas.

The CONAIE leader also said that

the unity and patience of the indigenous movement showed that it is possible to have a totally peaceful uprising to bring about changes. He also begged for the life of colonel Lucio Gutiérrez, arrested and incommunicado since Saturday, and for other rebel officers. 'We ask human rights organisations at national and international level to watch what happens in the country. We ourselves are expecting that if we continue our struggle they will harass us and arrest us,' he pleaded.

The new president Gustavo Noboa declared, after taking office, that he understood the indigenous demands, but that 'they used the wrong tactic to obtain their objectives, because of their desperation'. Noboa insisted that the insurgent colonels would have to be tried to serve as examples. 'We must have discipline, not with a heavy hand but firmness,' he said.

The new interior minister, Francisco Huerta, who a few days earlier had backed the indigenous movement and rejected dollarisation, abruptly changed his position and came out in favour of dollarisation. He said it was necessary to begin a dialogue with the indigenous movement but added: 'We are not going to cure the republic with witchcraft or hostile demonstrations. The potential of the indigenous cannot rest on shamanism or on alcohol. Our ethnic groups are equally important.'

In an indigenous community of Cotopaxi, two hours from Quito, the inhabitants, who had met to talk about the uprising, spoke of their unease at the outcome of the insurrection. Mauricio Chiliquinga said he was sad because after having achieved a popular government, 'in the end a solution was found that benefits the same old politicians and powerful men'.

Mariano Guzñai said Gustavo Noboa's government was 'more of the same' and did not inspire confidence. 'Noboa or Mahuad, it's all the same. They all must go because none of them cares about what happens to us or to the poor in this country. If they did care, they would have forgotten about the dollar [dollarisation] proposed by the rich,' he said. 'Our victory was a disaster, but now nothing frightens us. If before we fought to get back our land against the landowners who were exploiting us, now we will continue to struggle against politicians and bankers who are robbing us,' said Guzñai.

Journalist Paco Velasco, director of the Quito Radio La Luna, said he was worried by the fact that they are prosecuting the insurgent colonels, which will deepen even further the wound that has opened during the last few days. 'The indigenous and military rebels mounted an insurrection because they were desperate about so much corruption and poverty. They may have been mistaken in the method they used, but it was a just and idealistic struggle, which according to the polls, was backed by the great majority of the population,' he said.

Velasco believes a general amnesty is needed to heal the wounds and make it possible to go forward by permitting the return of the rebel officers to the army. 'Now many members of parliament, political and business leaders are burbling on about the defence of democracy, when they have done little or nothing to defend it. These people showed great selflessness in the defence of Ecuador, and now they are calling them insurgents who tried to carry out a coup,' he said.

According to the journalist, if all those who plotted coups in Ecuador

'If before we fought to get back our land against the landowners who were exploiting us, now we will continue to struggle against politicians and bankers who are robbing us'

were to be brought to account, this would have to include Mahuad, who was denounced for having been preparing a 'Fujimori-style coup'. 'They would also have to judge many politicians like ex-president León Febres Cordero, who made known that a coup was in preparation, but never did anything to stop it,' he argued. 'If they all have to be put in prison, this would also include the members of parliament who, after overthrowing Abdalá Bucaram in 1997, instead of proceeding with the presidential succession, named one of themselves, Fabián Alarcón, as interim president, trampling on the constitution,' argued Velasco.

He expressed doubts about the legality of the present government, nominated by the high military command and ratified by a majority in parliament. The ex-president had never resigned, and said that he was overthrown.

Jorge Loor, of the National Peasant Co-ordinating Committee, and one of those who took an active part in the recent protests, said that for the indigenous and peasant movement of Ecuador there were two governments. 'One with legitimacy represents the true Ecuador of the great majorities, which was manifested in the Junta of National Salvation,' he said. Loor believes there is also a government 'which calls itself legal and is presided over by Gustavo Noboa supported by the right-wing parties [Social Christian, Popular Democracy and Ecuadorian Roldosista], bankers and some businessmen.'

A dance of accusations
24 January 2000 (Monday)

Outwardly, the resilience of the indigenous and the fortitude of the colonels in the face of defeat contrast with an almost tragi-comic spectacle of politicians and journalists terrified at the 'nightmare' of having an indigenous in government. 'Imagine us having to speak Quechua,' said one confused former minister.

While such people are being turned into defenders of democracy and history is being forgotten, the indigenous maintain their dignity of 500 years. Some journalists of the international press who arrived in Quito smiled when they reported the parliamentary session of Saturday 22nd. 'How slippery these members of parliament are,' says a Brazilian colleague, and adds: 'It's difficult to find their like anywhere else.'

A journalist from Venezuela speaks of 'the lamentable role the television channels played, showing only one side of the coin,' and says: 'The image that stays with me is of chancellor Benjamín Ortíz, a journalist, accused of being involved in a coup.'

An Argentine writer says that the dance of accusations 'demonstrates the poverty of these types'. 'Mendoza accuses Mahuad, Gallardo and Ortíz of having proposed a Fujimori-type coup. Gallardo accuses Mendoza and the current chief of the joint command, Telmo Sandoval, of having been preparing a coup against Mahuad for some time. Febres Cordero says he knew a coup was in preparation. However, he did nothing to prevent it because he wanted Mahuad to go and Noboa to come in. The right-wing members of parliament accuse [general Paco] Moncayo of being a coup-maker because he supported the colonels and the indigenous movement, and he was dismissed. The parliament is a body in which no one believes, but it will be in charge of setting up dollarisation. The right-wing sectors in general say the coup was by the colonels and the indigenous movement, although they prefer to put the blame on the colonels and to avoid criticising the indigenous movement. For them democracy was restored with the presidential succession, although they do not say it was the high military command that decreed the dismissal of Mahuad to put in Noboa as president, even though Mahuad had not resigned. Moncayo says that [León] Febres Cordero, [Jaime] Nebot and [Fabián] Alarcón all asked him several times to perpetrate a coup against Abdalá Bucaram when he was chief of the joint command. He says they are hypocrites because at that time they had nothing to say against a coup and now they keep burbling on about democracy. The public prosecutor brought proceedings against Moncayo, Yandún, Vargas and Solórzano, but not against Mendoza or Telmo Sandoval. Ecuador is champion at breaking constitutions – if indeed one exists here at all – and saying that everything was done within a constitutional framework.' All in all, Macondo[30] is a joke.

Referendum and Indian reflections

25 January 2000 (Tuesday) The president of CONAIE, Antonio Vargas, warns of the risk of civil war if the new government does not take steps to help the most needy, and carries on with the same economic model as Jamil Mahuad. 'I don't want to frighten anyone but the reality is too overwhelming and the people are now tired of so much lying,' said Vargas.

Monsignor Luis Alberto Luna Tobar, archbishop of Cuenca, said he understands what Vargas is saying. 'The country is going through a civil war. It is not a war to the death, but it does prevent any possibility of response and development,' he said. The archbishop said the confrontation is not with fire-arms or primitive weapons but is a 'crueller war chemically planned by sick brains. These brains are sick with pseudo-democracy, pseudo-equality and pseudo-constitutionality. They have always neglected the poor and they have come out victorious.

'Among the strategies used in this war is the claim that the indigenous will gain in dollars through dollarisation, without understanding their language of needs and anxieties, or hunger and poverty,' he argued.

Luna Tobar stated that all political forces asked for Mahuad's dismissal and today some deny their involvement so that they can take part in the new government.

'I don't know when the government will be able to solve the social and economic problems, but it has a duty to do so. It is logical to say it will take six months; what is illogical is saying it can be done tomorrow,' he concluded.

[30] Macondo, the fictional town at the heart of Gabriel García Marquez's novel *100 Years of Solitude*, has become a by-word for the fantastic.

26 January 2000 (Wednesday) The indigenous movement has announced that it is prepared to talk with the government of Gustavo Noboa on condition that the authorities do not persecute the leaders of last week's insurrection. CONAIE is only waiting to be called by the government, said the organisation's president, Antonio Vargas.

Today Noboa receives the presidential sash in parliament after the overthrow of his predecessor, Jamil Mahuad.

Vargas has made it clear that if the government 'calls for a political truce, it must express itself in acts of full justice, fair economic and social policies and must not try to seek out the guilty among leaders and patriotic military'.

The authorities are insisting on punishing the rebel leaders who occupied parliament and the government house last Friday. The situation is being aggravated by the detention of the insurgent colonels and the request for the indictment and imprisonment of Vargas, Solórzano, the members of parliament Paco Moncayo and René Yandún as well as all the civilians identified as participants in the uprising.

Vargas is asking the supreme court to inform him when he must present himself for imprisonment. 'Here I am. I am not going to run away, because I am not a banker, not a businessman, not one of those who stole the people's money and ran off to the US,' he says. He argues that in order to imprison all those who took part in the uprising, gigantic prisons will have to be built 'because there are millions of us in the country and the towns'.

Colonel Gutiérrez, leader of the revolt, is known to be in prison, as are his peers Celso Andrade and Jorge Brito. Legal proceedings have been started against 300 officers who supported the insurrection. This has created more division in military ranks, because as well as the large numbers being brought to court, these officers are popular with the troops, they have distinguished themselves as leaders and they have good qualifications.

'Unfortunately, what has happened has weakened the army as an institution,' which is 'in a very delicate situation,' said the new defence minister, retired admiral Hugo Unda. He says the army insurgents will be tried by martial law. Their personal safety and their legitimate right to a defence will be guaranteed.

Noboa accepts that the crisis affecting 'the great majorities' caused the 'popular non-conformity', which is 'accentuated among the indigenous people' and 'deserves attention' urgently.

CONAIE has proposed to the new government that it should call a plebiscite at the same time as the municipal elections on 21 May, to ask whether the citizenry accepts Noboa as president, and on dollarisation and the privatisations proposed by Mahuad, which the new government plans to proceed with, said Vargas.

Paco Moncayo has declared that 'a witch hunt' has been started against the insurgents, which 'is evidence of the fear felt by powerful groups' and may have 'very unfortunate consequences for the country. This is the vengeance of a mentally and spiritually sick right-wing, who are trying to get over their fright at seeing the people with the capacity to gain power.'

Moncayo is proposing to the social movements that they get up a petition and collect signatures to ask for 'the annulment of the mandate of this parliament'.

Archbishop Luis Alberto Luna Tobar, says only forgiveness can heal the wounds 'which are not new, but have grown deeper with the present economic situation and may become even worse if solutions are not sought through dialogue'.

Analysts say that only dialogue between the government and the indigenous organisation and civil society can prevent the hardening of the antagonisms that provoked the popular uprising last week. They believe the crisis that led to the insurrection continues to simmer and is threatening to break out in renewed conflict.

The editorial of the Quito daily, *El Comercio*, warns of the danger of a social breakdown if the new government goes ahead with its dollarisation plan, and does not listen to the indigenous movement. 'Dollarisation not only aligned the elites. It became the symbol for the indigenous and social movements of a system which they are not prepared to tolerate,' according to *El Comercio*, the most important newspaper in the Ecuadorian capital. Dollarisation has become a dividing line between the social movements and 'a large part of the power elites' said the editorial. 'Setting the clock right is painful. But neither the elites who support dollarisation, nor the government have said how – and when – they are thinking of making a social pact with the marginalised of the country.' *El Comercio* said that if no action is taken in this direction, 'the country's social disintegration may grow worse and become a breeding ground for irrational and extremist activities.'

28 January 2000 (Friday) The national assembly of CONAIE, consisting of representatives of different indigenous nations and peoples, met today to reflect on the popular insurrection. Serenity, despite the defeat. 'Our road is long, it does not come to an end in one day, and this was an advance along the road,' said Antonio Vargas.

For the president of CONAIE, that small step along a centuries-long road is also a gigantic one. 'Sometimes the *mestizos* are in too much of a hurry and believe that things can be achieved by a march broken up by police. Things are achieved with time,' comments Vargas.

The assembly described the actions of 21 January in different provinces, with occupations of town halls and government buildings, as happened in Carchi, Cotopaxi, Bolívar, Azuay, Guayas, the taking of oil wells in Napo and road blocks all over the country. For the participants the mobilisation in Quito was also a success. Nevertheless, questions were raised. Some wondered if it wasn't unrealistic to march on the government house. Others wondered whether it would not have been better to stay in the parliament building and negotiate from a position of strength for a public consultation with the new president. Others believe it was a mistake to negotiate with the high command when it had never demonstrated its clear opposition to the system. Others say the indigenous mobilisation may have been used to get rid of Mahuad, and the outcome was the one that rightwing sectors and the US embassy wanted. Some questioned CONAIE's long-time use of a certain person as an adviser, who was ethically dubious because he was too closely linked to police as a 'grass'. Some wanted the Pachakutik members of parliament to

'Our road is long, it does not come to an end in one day, and this was an advance along the road,'

resign. Others said this would mean losing a political space they had won. There is an atmosphere of self-criticism among the Indians, of reflection and a firm intention of rescuing everything positive from their defeat. They were determined to strengthen the iron unity that was demonstrated in the mobilisations of 1999 and over the past few weeks.

But beyond the mistakes, the insurrection of 21 January confirms something that all governments think, but do not put into practice: Ecuador cannot manage without the indigenous movement.

The assembly resolved to ask Gustavo Noboa to call a popular consultation for 21 May, when local elections take place and 'thus affirm democracy'. The questions CONAIE is asking are: Are you in agreement with the sovereign will of the people that on 21 January determined the dismissal of president Jamil Mahuad and with the suspension of members of parliament and the ministers of the supreme court of justice? Do you agree that Ecuador should maintain its monetary sovereignty and that the *sucre* should continue to be the official currency, and that dollarisation should be dropped? Do you agree with the immediate return of frozen deposits at the value at which they were frozen? Do you agree with the repatriation of ill-gotten money and the indictment of the bankers who have harmed the state and benefited illegally from public resources? Do you agree that the state, in exercise of its sovereignty, should maintain control, management and ownership of oil, electricity, telecommunications and social security, that the plan of the Auditor's Commission and all privatisation processes should be stopped?

'If you want democracy so much, then return sovereignty to the people in a popular consultation and show that you are true democrats,' says Miguel Lluco. 'If it is true that the authority of authorities comes from the people then you must place yours at the people's disposal.'

If Noboa does not agree to hold a plebiscite, CONAIE and the social movements will collect around 600,000 signatures to conduct a referendum, in what may be a new challenge for the indigenous and social movements of Ecuador.

LORI WASELCHUK

PART 2

BETWEEN VOICES: INTERVIEWS

MAURICIO USHIÑA

Words are like old animals lurking in the memory. The memory is like a labyrinth where ancient words summon ghosts. Words are traded on the human market. We are seeking the place where the meanings have remained hidden, to rescue the ethical principles that once were the very essence of social relationships. Let us listen to the voices behind the volcanoes, and with them to the word.

ANDRES GUERRERO

The indigenous and the constitutional myth

Andrés Guerrero is a sociologist well known outside his native Ecuador. He gained his master's degree in sociology at the University of Paris and has done research in various Latin American and European countries. He is visiting professor of the Latin American Faculty of Social Sciences. He has published various books on the lives of peasants and indigenous of Ecuador, with whom he lived for a long time. Among his most important works are: *The Huasipunguero Peasantry in Ecuador. The Pre-capitalist Hacienda in Ecuador, Peasant-indigenous Reproduction Strategies* and *From Economics to Attitudes: Agrarian Structures and Conflicts.* In his most recent book *The Semantics of Domination: Dealing with Indians* he investigates rural problems connected with agrarian reform in Ecuador. For some years he has been investigating the relationships of domination through different Ecuadorian constitutions and the relation between the laws of the country and the real lives of the indigenous.

A constant theme in your research has been relationships of domination in the indigenous world? What were you seeking to prove in your work?

I was interested to find out how very strong relationships of ethnic domination were established (from the time of Ecuador's constitution as a republic), although they were covered up by the 'Constitution of a Republic of Free and Equal Citizens'. Ecuador follows the models of the French and US revolutions, which are based on a state of free citizens living together in 'freedom and equality'. Homogeneity is also marked, as all the citizens must be culturally equal and that's where the problem begins.

Is it possible to say that the constitution of Ecuador has been a work of fiction?

The myth of the constitution served to set up a national state called Ecuador, in a territory belonging to the royal *Audiencia* of Quito, with a population that had been calling itself Ecuadorian since 1830.

My research aimed to discover in what way this founding myth (the constitution of the republic) covered over unequal power relations since, 170 years later, you go out on the street and find that the 'homogeneous, free, equal Ecuadorian citizen' does not exist. There are not only class differences, which are in some way foreseen in the constitution, when it lays down that 'citizens may be different with respect to wealth'. But the country is made up of whites and Indians and the constitution not only covered up but also reproduced relationships of ethnic domination. The indigenous organisations showed us the reality that the national state of 'free and equal' citizens was a myth.

How is this fiction constructed?

When reform of the constitution is discussed as if it was going to change a social, economic and symbolic reality, then the fiction is being constructed.

Whereas the constitution is something abstract which tries to formulate the ideal of society that some want to attain, the administrative laws are more pragmatic. They regulate the immediate in order to make it become reality. The interesting thing is that the administrative part does not consider the existence of the citizen. That is to say, at no time are the citizens consulted about whether a law should be adopted or not. It is adopted without anyone being able to discuss it. Whereas a referendum is called to change something abstract like the constitution, a law can be passed on the spur of the moment, which may actually change some very important matters. There is no democratic system if on the one hand we maintain citizenship as an *abstract* right and on the other hand, we have an administration of the population that deals in the *reality* of the relationship between the state and the population.

Do you think the indigenous movement is bringing these two any closer?

When the indigenous demand pluri-nationality and say that they want another type of political structure, in which they belong as citizens who are different, with their own nations, they are up against the historical process, which associated citizenship with the administration of the population. Up until now this administration has tried to undermine the functioning of indigenous organisations, because they claim the communal system as an essential point. I don't want to idealise the communal system at all, but it is a crucial element claimed by indigenous organisations.

Let's talk a little about what the community means in cultural and symbolic terms.

For the indigenous the community is something mythological. In the domestic, inter-domestic and partially communal spheres, relationships of solidarity exist which are not commercial. This creates a political, cultural and symbolic cohesion. Some people think it would be better if the indigenous stopped thinking this way and became buyers and sellers. The indigenous know how to manage very well in two codes: the commercial code for the outside world and the code of reciprocity and communal solidarity at home. If the communal aspect comes to an end, solidarity disintegrates. If forms of solidarity disintegrate a situation of generalised violence might occur.

ANTONIO VARGAS

A bombshell for the politicians

Antonio Vargas is a native of the Amazonian province of Pastaza. He belongs to the Quechua nation and was leader of the Pastaza Indigenous Peoples' Organisation (OPIP). He became president of the Confederation of the Indigenous Nations of Ecuador (CONAIE) in 1996, when it was suffering from a sharp divide between the Amazonian organisations and those of the Sierra. This division was encouraged by the government of the then president Abdalá Bucaram. Vargas was re-elected at the congress held in November 1999, gaining a few votes over Ricardo Ulcuango, then president of ECUARUNARI. Ulcuango was unanimously elected vice-president. During his period at the head of CONAIE, Vargas has sought to maintain unity in the indigenous movement and wanted its decisions to be shared by ECUARUNARI. He was an important factor in the alliance between the indigenous movement and progressive army officers during the popular rebellion of January 2000 and he was the indigenous person to have come closest to the presidency when he formed part of the Junta of National Salvation.

What did the recent indigenous uprising achieve?

For the indigenous movement, all the uprisings since 1990 have served to show Ecuador and the world that a marginalised people, who had been left behind, have decided to fight for their rights and build a different country. We believe we accomplished the objective of sacking the three powers. But above all, we have placed at the centre of the debate the bad reputation those powers have in society. Many people said it was a dream, it was suicide, it was madness on the part of the indigenous leaders and we proved them wrong. Despite the apartheid to which our brothers and sisters were subjected when all who were wearing ponchos were chucked off the buses by the military, they still arrived on foot. And the important thing is that there was great unity in the different actions we carried out.

So wasn't it a defeat?

Not at all, because it not only helped strengthen the indigenous movement but also increased the unity between Ecuadorians who want changes. It also made people realise that this struggle is not just an Indian struggle but everybody's struggle.

Since last July CONAIE has become the axis of unity between the social sectors and the indigenous world. Perhaps it was a mistake to have been able to socialise our political plan a lot more, but it is true that the press hit us hard.

Did you feel used at any time during the uprising?

What we do is the fruit of our own reflections and we never let ourselves be used. Sometimes discrepancies arise with some sectors who want to advance in a great hurry and this haste results in a few little marches and confrontations with the police without achieving anything, because the government has got them taped.

How did the media hit you hard?

They tried to make us quarrel between ourselves by giving space to certain leaders who do not represent anyone. They wanted to exacerbate our differences and open wounds. They also issued a clearly falsified document purporting to be signed by Salvador Quiste and saying, 'Checkmate to the *mestizos*'. They never give the same space afterwards to the denial. They also criticised the fact that some of our comrades painted some people,[31] which is not right, but the media had nothing to say when these same comrades were ordered off buses, or when they were greeted with teargas bombs last July.

[31] On 20 January 2000, the indigenous had surrounded the congress building and were stopping people passing. They seized some people who attempted to pass the blockade and painted their faces in indigenous ceremonial style and made them dance. This was heavily criticised by the mainstream media, which said it was a form of racism against whites.

What is the importance of your alliance with officers of the armed forces?

This is very important because a new type of soldier is appearing who sees that change is possible. These new soldiers offer a hope that does not exist among the generals, because they are more involved in corruption and defend their own interests. It is a seed, and one day there will be a change throughout the armed forces. As with the officers and troops, the support of priests and nuns was very important to us, even though the top of the Church was not with us.

MAURICIO USHÑA

Antonio Vargas (seated on the right) addressing the National Parliament of the Peoples of Ecuador, January 2000.

Wasn't it a mistake to rush off to take the government palace and leave the parliament building uncovered?

There was a lot of pressure from people who wanted to go and take over the presidency, because it was another important symbol of corruption, together with the parliament and the supreme court. Perhaps it was a mistake and if we had remained in the parliament building the outcome would have been different. But this needs to be analysed and in any case, what has happened has happened. When we arrived at Carondelet, the generals had a proclamation prepared and a telegram in which they announced that they were assuming all power. We did not accept it and so we talked. Perhaps it was a mistake to allow Mendoza to be part of the junta, but if we had not, a lot of blood would have flowed. Meanwhile, some members of parliament, frightened to death, were preparing to hold the parliament in Guayaquil.

'Our struggle is not for power itself. There are many more important things than power for its own sake, such as society changing from within'

What does having been so close to power mean to the indigenous people?

Our struggle is not for power itself. There are many more important things than power for its own sake, such as society changing from within, starting to create more vivid and colourful days, and starting to understand that there must be a change. Of course when you are moving towards changes it is necessary that there should also be change from within the government. An enduring lesson is that we carried out an uprising which came close to power, but if we had been determined to cling on to power there would have been confrontations and deaths. We decided to give another way a chance. The important thing is that we have caused a shake-up in the political class. We made it clear that we were a people in rebellion who want changes without violence.

Will this shake-up lead to changes in such racist politicians?

I think there will be changes in attitude, at least for some. They will have to take into account that the majority is against them and they can't go on just doing things their way without seeking alternatives. Likewise, we will have to go on fighting to achieve our objective.

What do you expect from Gustavo Noboa's government?

If this government has the will to make changes, it can do so without any problems. That is, if it does not go the same way as Mahuad and build its own tomb. If it thinks that we just want some small agreements for our communities, then the government has no idea of what is happening. What we want is much deeper, we are not beggars asking for handouts. The authorities are supposed to be enlightened people, but in practice they are often ignorant and don't understand the people's situation, so they fail miserably.

What will CONAIE's relationship be with the indigenous legislators?

We will have to see how things go. I believe their experience is also very valid but it is not salvation. We have to look at things long term and so we have to find different solutions, experiences like the provincial parliaments, which are being set up as a kind of check on the authorities. Our legislators should be much more closely linked to the indigenous movement and to society in general, but often they are absorbed by the system.

How do you see the future?

Hope for the future means struggling and not becoming discouraged. In a while change is going to happen – change that will arrive without violence, peacefully, involving the communities. What has happened has been a test for us. It made people feel in their hearts that it could be done, that we don't have to stay quiet, because that is a way of serving the same old politicians. Violent struggle does not lead to much. Mobilising large masses through organisation is the best way to get changes. Of course if these changes don't come, then violence might result, but we always have to tread carefully so that this does not happen. We have to move patiently so that it does not come to this. But we must be aware that in the future there may be a big social explosion, even a civil war. People may go out looting if they have nothing to eat.

LUIS MACAS

Ushay, power, is a collective concept

Luis Macas belongs to the Saraguro people, one of those making up the Quechua nation. He was a founder and president of CONAIE, and a member of parliament for the Pachakutik Movement for Pluri-national Unity – New Country. At the time of this interview he was director of the Scientific Institute for Indigenous Cultures. He took an active part in the organisations and actions in the 1990 uprising, which marked the breakthrough of the indigenous into modern political life, and in many mobilisations led by CONAIE. Naturally he was with his brothers and sisters in the insurrection of January 2000.

What significance does the recent indigenous uprising have?

It means that Latin American history from its first inhabitants onwards is present. That the invasion from the West did not complete its mission to liquidate the indigenous peoples. It is obvious that Indian resistance through various mechanisms of struggle is alive and active. The uprising of the indigenous movement and the popular movements is firm proof that there is a crisis and that the problem of justice and fairness, ethics and morality have not been solved by the current democracy and political system. That is to say, this uprising is a cry to the world that the situation in Ecuador and other Latin American countries has not been resolved. It is also a summons to all people for us to create a *minga* of actions and proposals by the sectors who are really suffering the effects of the neoliberal model, to find common solutions.

LORI WASELCHUK

Luis Macas talking to the media, January 2000.

What is the future of the indigenous movement after the insurrection?

From the political space the indigenous movement has gained through its historical struggles, its fundamental task, was, is and will be to help resolve the problems that afflict the people of Ecuador. That is to say, our struggles have begun fights for fundamental changes, such as what we were demanding in this uprising: to re-establish the country by breaking with the old structures of the state and the political system, which are worn out.

When you took part in the setting up of CONAIE, was this with the purpose of gaining power, or did that come as you went along?

At the same time as we were organising to build the unity of our peoples, obtain fundamental rights for our communities and improve living conditions, both at individual and collective level, we were always aware that the state we are living in does not respond to the needs of the majority of the population. That is why we in the indigenous movement and the social movements spoke of building a different state, a pluri-national state. This means recognising ourselves, and recognising our differences, an important factor in creating harmony between Ecuadorians.

What does power mean for the indigenous?

For the indigenous world, power, *ushay*, means perfecting living conditions, it is a collective concept. It is the capacity to develop collectively, with each making his or her own distinct contribution, as happens in the *minga*, in which children, women and old people each have a role. Every role is important in society.

What difference or likeness is there between the 1990 uprising and the recent one?

The 1990 uprising demonstrated to the country and the world that we indigenous peoples had not disappeared. And above all, we showed that we were in a position to be protagonists in society, making contributions and proposals from our own point of view. We proved that we Caras, Panzaleos, Puruhaes, Cañaris are present in this country with our ancestral wisdom, our music, our different colours. That we are not hidden in museums merely as archaeological or anthropological objects of study, just to recall the history that patriotic sentimentalists tell in their stories. The uprising at the beginning of 2000 shows that we have been able to carry on through adversities, bringing proposals to summon all to make the changes that Ecuador needs. In the time between 1990 and 2000 we reflected deeply, not only internally about the indigenous peoples, but on the global reality of our society, and this has forced us to take decisions and confront problems.

What symbolic significance does democracy have for the indigenous peoples?

Although the term democracy does not exist in the language of [Ecuador's] indigenous peoples, we have something more profound, which is reciprocity and solidarity, which are the fundamental principles for living together in harmony in society. That is why we understand democracy must be rooted in justice, fairness and harmony. The search for consensus leads us to come to agreements, but above all to dialogue and reflection in order to reach a consensus. These are the processes by which our peoples and communities work. That is why the democracy operated by the logic of those who hold power is not understood by indigenous people. How can we understand that in the distribution of wealth, 20 per cent of the population benefits and 80 per cent is left in poverty? This would never be accepted in a community and we cannot accept that it should happen in the country. That is why from our state of poverty we have raised our voice and rebelled against those who have robbed the wealth of our peoples.

Is the alliance with progressive sectors of the armed forces a priority or should it be taken as a general part of the movement's alliances?

Our alliances with progressive sectors of society and the armed forces are a necessity in the indigenous peoples' struggle, but this alliance is based on identifying structural problems, resolving them and building a different state. I believe that this is also the soldiers' struggle, which is why they identified with the indigenous peoples.

When they announce sanctions and want to punish those who took part in the uprising, are they polarising Ecuadorian society?

Of course, from the point of view of 'justice' they have got to teach a lesson, give correction to those 'guilty' of this revolt. From our viewpoint, it is a great opportunity to understand the scope of the problem that our country is experiencing, because those who rose up to establish justice are the 'guilty' ones and the ones the state is out to punish. This fact will bring the people together and above all it will raise the consciousness of our peoples. The state will end up with its 'justice' and we will unite all the more to put an end to injustice.

'the democracy operated by the logic of those who hold power is not understood by indigenous people. How can we understand that in the distribution of wealth, 20 per cent of the population benefits and 80 per cent is left in poverty? This would never be accepted in a community and we cannot accept that it should happen in the country'

What has happened to the indigenous movement's electoral participation since the insurrection?

This is just another front to fight on. It is not the final objective. That is why we will go out as ever with our proposals for change to compete with the political parties, which are just electoral businesses offering money. We are offering our struggle and our way of looking at things.

What can the indigenous movement expect from the government that replaced Jamil Mahuad's?

Mahuad's government represented the banking sector and certain businesses from the Sierra. Now Noboa's government and the constitution of his cabinet also represents those same sectors, but with the stress on the Ecuadorian coast. That is to say, it is a continuation of the previous government, since there is absolutely no change in its policies and it will continue with Mahuad's plans, such as dollarisation and privatisation. Neither will corruption be eradicated. This makes us think that for the indigenous peoples and the Ecuadorian people as a whole, there has not been much change.

NINA PACARI

Plurality does not mean division

1

Since 1996, the indigenous of Ecuador have been taking part in elections through the Pachakutik Pluri-national Movement – New Country, a movement that draws them together with non-governmental organisations, ecologists, women's groups and various social organisations. The candidate for each municipality is nominated after a long assembly in which local communities take part. The same system is used in the provinces and at national level.

In the 1998 elections the list of members elected to the national parliament was headed by Nina Pacari, who was elected by a substantial majority. Pacari belongs to the Quechua nation. She was born in 1961 in Cotacachi, in the province of Imbabura. She is a lawyer and was the head of lands and territories in the Confederation of Indigenous Nations of Ecuador (CONAIE). In 1997 she was appointed president of the National Planning Council for Indigenous and Black Peoples (CONPLADEIN), which was set up to formulate state policies on indigenous and black peoples, as well as planning and carrying out development projects. This later became the Council of Nations and Peoples of Ecuador (CODENPE).

In November 1997 she was elected to the national parliament. When the new parliament sat, in August 1998, she was elected vice-president, an office never before held by an indigenous person. 'For the indigenous movement, this event is historic, because until now not a single indigenous comrade, much less a woman, had ever held any office in parliament,' says Pacari. But the fact of having gained the vice-presidency shifted the ground a bit within the country, because we are not accustomed to seeing an indigenous woman leading such an important body as the parliament. It also had an impact internationally. Ecuador must get used to seeing indigenous, men and women occupying decision-making posts, without losing their identity or their commitment to the sectors they represent.

2

When she came to assess the performance of the indigenous mayors elected in the 1998 municipal election, Pacari singled out an administration that was given as an example by different sectors in the country: Guamote, in the province of Chimborazo. 'There, 98 per cent of the population is indigenous, which means that in a sense they all aimed towards a common project, but obviously without excluding the *mestizo* minority,' she says. 'There, cantonal development committees are being organised with participation by citizens. They also hold assemblies where representatives from the communities analyse the municipal budget, set priorities and control and keep track of investments. With this participative form of management, not only is the municipality democratised, but they succeed in optimising the few resources that come to the Town Hall from central government. Co-management enables them to do many more things than those stipulated in the budget.'

In Cotacachi, where the indigenous

population is not in such a large majority as in Guamote, the performance of the indigenous mayor contributed towards dissolving the frontiers with the white *mestizo* world. 'The mayor is carrying out his administration on behalf of all the inhabitants with a very high level of participation from businessmen, artisans, non-indigenous women, together with our own indigenous communities,' says Pacari. 'The administration has succeeded in increasing integration with the non-indigenous and also increasing non-indigenous respect for our brothers and sisters. The assemblies that plan cantonal development are attended by all kinds of people and this large-scale participation of all sectors helped to single out the greatest needs and how to address them. These two models of participation and joint management in local government can serve for the country as a whole. It is part of the indigenous contribution to Ecuadorian society.'

3

Parliament is a very complex body in which many interests play a part. However, the indigenous are taking a chance that their proposals can develop in that environment. 'The scene in parliament is different from that at the level of the autonomous local powers, but it is still important for the development of the indigenous proposal,' Pacari says. 'We want an input not only on social matters but also economic, where we have presented our alternatives.'

In the previous session, the indigenous members of parliament gave an example of positive input, when they presented various bills of interest to the rural areas, like the creation of the Rural Financial Corporation (CORFINCA), but unfortunately they were not discussed. 'There is no guarantee that the same thing won't happen again. We need to strike agreements that will enable our proposals to be carried out, but above all we need to make sure public opinion knows about them. We have the task of expressing the indigenous voice and that of the popular sectors in parliament, even though we are in a minority.'

Asked whether the indigenous leaders were not risking becoming bureaucrats in parliament, she says that everything must be done to ensure this does not happen, and she stresses: 'Although members of parliament cannot be in the indigenous organisation, they must not lose their link and coordination with it. On the one hand, they must constantly visit the communities and on the other they must create mechanisms to express their wishes. My advisory team operates in three fundamental areas: one concerned with social organisation, another with structural politics and a third which is pre-eminently technical. In organisational politics, the indigenous organisations' proposals are articulated and defended in parliament. A team is working full time on these proposals through workshops and meetings, preparing to present them in parliament. The same happens with the subject of women. We, as members of parliament, get involved in a process and receive the proposals that come from the social movements. The

'Ecuador must get used to seeing indigenous, men and women occupying decision-making posts, without losing their identity or their commitment to the sectors they represent.'

PAUL SMITH / PANOS PICTURES

structural politics team is linked to Pachakutik, which is the guiding political movement to which we are answerable. The technical team is the support mechanism for getting things done inside parliament.'

Nina Pacari plays down the importance of certain regional divisions between indigenous of the Sierra and Amazonia, or political differences which sometimes occur in the indigenous movement. She points out that the unity of CONAIE has become stronger. 'Indigenous people are not uniform. We are 11 nations with different visions, processes and strategies, which depend partly on our geographical environment. For example, we cannot expect the same demands to be made in Amazonia as in the Sierra. Nevertheless, although we respect our differences, we are beginning to reach some consensus. We have to realise

that the fact that there are different views within the movement does not mean division but plurality.'

4

Since 1992 Ecuador's indigenous nations have achieved great gains. On the one hand, 80 per cent of land conflicts are being resolved; on the other, they have managed to insert pluri-nationality into the national debate, including intercultural bilingual education, and the cultural and legal plurality of the country. 'The new constitution recognised the collective rights of peoples, and the pluri-ethnic and multicultural character of the country,' says Pacari. 'In the case of indigenous medicine its right to be practise was recognised. One of the regulations lays down that indigenous medicine can count on state support for development resources. Before the constitutional reforms were recognised, our *yachas* or shamans were persecuted and sent to prison, but now they are not. In fact, rules need to be laid down to control abuses committed by non-indigenous people who say they are using our medicine.'

Parallel with the constitutional reforms there was the approval of Agreement 169 of the International Labour Organisation (ILO), which recognises the rights of indigenous peoples. 'Its approval by parliament in the previous session was a most important achievement for the indigenous movement, because it gave us legal bases. Now it has been established that judges who deal with offences committed by indigenous defendants have a duty to take into account indigenous norms, customs and culture, as mitigating factors when sentencing. Moreover, it has been recognised that, through their own authorities, our people can exercise legal powers, resolve conflicts and administer justice in accordance with our tradition. Thus, the simultaneous exercise of indigenous law is beginning to be recognised. It is therefore necessary, in this respect, to harmonise laws and establish levels of competence, so that indigenous and national laws do not conflict or contradict each other. The recognition of the indigenous legal system is a fundamental contribution to the development of their own daily life in the communities and to the resolution of many internal conflicts. The official use of indigenous languages is also recognised and the state has undertaken to respect it. If an indigenous person has to make a statement or application in a public office and does not speak Spanish, there is a duty to attend to him in his own language.'

According to Pacari, indigenous rules relate to the three basic principles of not lying, not stealing and not killing. Justice is collective, and the process always starts in a family council, then goes to a community council. After that it passes to the town council, and it is the whole community that decides on the sentence after the verdict. The punishment or sanction imposed by the indigenous, she says, always relates to a bodily and spiritual cleansing.

Pacari is confident about the future. She stresses that it is an important step that the new constitution says: The indigenous peoples who define themselves as nations are a constitutive part of the Ecuadorian state. In this way the indigenous nations are accepted. 'A state that involves this participation is going to become a pluri-national state and this must be evident both at institutional and structural level – with a parliament, for example, that allows for the representation of different peoples. Now there are indigenous in parliament, mainly Quechua, but this does not amount to pluri-ethnic representation. It has nothing to do with that – ours is unity in diversity. After the uniformity of the 1980s, we have passed to pluri-ethnicity, multiculturalism. Perhaps in a few years' time Ecuador will be able to call itself pluri-national. Let's hope that our experience in local government and in parliament contributes towards the construction of a pluri-national state, whose structure and administration demonstrate the country's plurality, involving indigenous and black peoples.'

INTERVIEW # MIGUEL LLUCO

In *minga* for life

Miguel Lluco Tixe is one of the founders of CONAIE, and took an active part in the uprising of 1990, when the movement began to advance towards the political arena. In 1995 he took part in the creation of the Pachakutik Movement for Pluri-national Unity – New Country, which carried him into parliament a year later, where he remained until 1998.

Lluco also took part in the occupation of Quito Cathedral, which was the prelude to the popular mobilisation of February 1997, that led to the sacking of Abdalá Bucaram from the government. The First National Pachakutik Congress, in August 1999, confirmed him unanimously as president of the organisation's national executive committee.

'We have to be protagonists of change, subjects not objects.'

The ethnic element and the demand for Ecuador to become a pluri-national country were, in principle, the factors that united the different indigenous ethnic groups. But you people have carried your activities beyond the limits of the indigenous world.

Ecuador's plural nature is demonstrated when the indigenous emerge as a protagonist in socio-political life. Then it is recognised that the "other" exists and they have their differences and their rights. It was then that CONAIE decided to seek alliances with other social organisations and independent trade unions to create the Pachakutik Movement in 1995.

The importance of Pachakutik is that it was born to represent the social movements without the protection of any political party. This factor united both indigenous and non-indigenous peoples around an alternative political project.

The essence of Pachakutik is unity in diversity. Within it there are city workers, non-indigenous peasants, ecologists, Afro-Ecuadorian sectors and indigenous.

Has its participation in elections been positive for the indigenous movement?

The participation of social organisations from both country and town in the electoral process enabled us to discover how far this activity would get us, and watching how traditional politicians behave.

It has shown us that in order to carry forward our most vital demands and aspirations, what is essential is vigilant participation by organised social sectors to give constant support to its representatives.

But sometimes popular participation does not happen because people don't take enough interest.

Our task is to show them [the popular sectors] that their work is not done just by going out to vote – that democracy is not just the vote and that this [passive] way of acting is a form of submission. Participation means that we have to create, to produce politics. We have to be protagonists of change, subjects not objects. We have to realise that as inhabitants of this country, we have obligations and rights, and one of these rights consists in demanding that those who represent us maintain their dignity. And if they don't maintain their dignity, the population must mobilise to revoke their mandate, as happened in the case of Abdalá Bucaram or Jamil Mahuad.

But people can get tired…

…of being called upon to participate so much? That's true, but that is why we must always be vigilant. Ecuadorians must realise that the exercise of citizenship does not mean waiting to be called, but acting when it is necessary. We must not let corruption and policies against the poorest section of the population get through easily.

You took action to change a despised and worn-out government like Bucaram's, then were defrauded by the new president Fabián Alarcón? Don't the people have the right to feel used?

Yes, they do. But, in spite of everything, February [1997] marked a fundamental event in our country's history, because the population showed it was not asleep, that there were millions of Ecuadorian men and women, without distinction of class or party, who were concerned about the fate of the country.

The people wanted change. Nevertheless, looking at it in perspective, we can see that only the people changed, the structures remained. That's the mistake. But the responsibility for this was not the people's but their leaders'.

'the exercise of citizenship does not mean waiting to be called, but acting when it is necessary'

You took part in the takeover of the Cathedral (in Quito) and in the solution agreed by parliament to dismiss Bucaram, and later you fought against the corruption of Alarcón's government.

I take responsibility for what I did. At the time I too believed that the solution that occurred was the only possible one. Perhaps if we had sought another [solution] outside the traditional political parties, things would have turned out differently and I would not have had to denounce the corruption. The people's courage in rising up, and the mandate that gave, was mocked by the traditional politicians.

'Now, of course there is sadness. How can there not be? The loser is not the indigenous movement but the country, even though these same media and the same old politicians want people to think the opposite.'

And with Mahuad? To get so close, just in order for a change for happen that was not the one wanted by the popular movement?

When the military authorities came on the scene, I had doubts as to whether they would be free to come out on the side of the people – some of the generals, who in many cases are distant from the real, deep Ecuador. And indeed in the end they showed their slipperiness. The behaviour of many officers and other ranks was very different. They are always closer to the indigenous people and so they are more aware of their needs and they know about our people's hardships. These were the ones who had the courage to join the indigenous and popular protest, without being afraid of reprisals they might suffer, which in fact they are suffering at this moment.

Isn't there frustration at the outcome of the uprising?

I wouldn't call it frustration because we demonstrated our power to mobilise, which other people might envy. The indigenous movement demonstrated that it has great strength, because it can mobilise tens of thousands of people and paralyse the country. What's more, it demonstrated the cohesion of its leadership. These two things give it a power that other indigenous movements of the continent lack. We came out peacefully to change the corruption entrenched in the government and we were joined by military police, church people, small businessmen, students, common citizens. Never before have we achieved such a broad and democratic social agreement. That was why we remained massively in force on the streets and roads for more than a week. We succeeded in unmasking the government's hypocrisy. Then through the popular parliaments in the provinces and the Parliament of the Peoples of Ecuador concrete alternative proposals were worked out. Even though the mass media did not report them, that does not mean they were not there.

Now, of course there is sadness. How can there not be? The loser is not the indigenous movement but the country, even though these same media and the same old politicians want people to think the opposite.

Wasn't it naïve to trust the military authorities?

Perhaps, but it is also true that events happened at a very giddy pace and I believe that if the colonels had not accepted the command of the top brass that Mendoza should be part of the junta, much blood might have flowed, and our protest was and is a peaceful one. Our protest is based on active non-violence. We could not have endured having dead people on our hands. At any rate, it also succeeded in unmasking the crafty top brass of the country's military. This has made it even clearer that, on one side, there are the people and those who fight against corruption, and on the other, the corrupt. The uprising's peaceful character is also a magnificent demonstration, which the Ecuadorian media failed to highlight.

Do you consider the uprising was an attack on the democratic system?

You have only to look at what Doctor Mahuad's government was, and how unpopular it had become to realise that that is a lie. You have to see the disgraceful process of impoverishment into which he led us, demonstrated by the massive emigration of our fellow-countrymen – and not a few have died for this reason – and the shameful number of beggars, the alarming growth of delinquency. All this is in obedience to the caprice of Doctor Mahuad in ruling the country and supporting a group of corrupt bankers, who carried off nearly two international monetary reserves.[32] This led to the freezing of deposits belonging to thousands of Ecuadorians; thousands of Ecuadorians lost their life's savings and we are all paying for their incompetence and roguery through galloping inflation. Roguery which attempted to culminate in a process of dollarisation and privatisation, which will put an end once and for all to the national patrimony and sovereignty of Ecuador. None of this could have occurred without the complicity of parliament and the supreme court.

The banker Aspiazu gave US$2 million for the electoral campaign of the running mates Mahuad-Noboa. How much more corrupt money did this pair receive in order to win the elections? Will we ever know? Will there ever be an end to this electoral farce that those who have money win the elections? How can we trust a justice system headed by the principal suspect in the oil bonanza of the 1970s?

[32] This is a reference to bankers who were in control of the banks that collapsed through bad management of their capital assets, funds being diverted to parallel companies. After declaring themselves bankrupt, these same banks were assisted by Mahuad's government.

'we are open to dialogue, but not to a dialogue of fools, in which they talk to us after they have already taken all the decisions'

Certain politicians and media accuse you of being coup-makers...

It has been proved that corruption is deep-rooted throughout the present government. In the face of this, the social and indigenous movement and some concerned army officers could not remain silent and indolent. That is why we set up a junta of national salvation, which could have put a stop to the corruption of the powerful and established a development model that would have ended shameful poverty. We were betrayed by a crafty military high command, who betrayed their own honour rather than the popular sectors, who were simply acting as a channel for the discontent.

But it is right to point out that before us there were others who intended to break up the constitutional order. Mahuad himself planned his own coup, according to general Mendoza. There was an unconstitutional freeze on the deposits of Ecuadorians, and finally there was a coup by the military high command, ratified by the national parliament. There are many coup-makers but the media prefer not to talk about them. We were not intransigent with Mahuad's regime. We exhausted all the mechanisms and spaces for negotiation, but we were never listened to and we did not want to repeat the mistake of February 1997, when after the dismissal of Bucaram, we handed over our struggle to the national parliament. Then the cure was worse than the disease when they installed Alarcón as president, although he was also accused of corruption.

What will happen to the Pachakutik Movement members in the national parliament who have placed their seats at the people's disposal?

For the moment they must stay on, because it is a legitimate space we have gained. Nobody gave it to us on a plate and it was not gained by bankers' money. These members of parliament are a public voice and although they are in a numerical minority, at least they can contribute to the debate.

What's more, if the government keeps up the same economic programme of dollarisation, which limits national sovereignty and increases poverty, we need to maintain the struggle in all possible arenas.

What is Pachakutik's position in relation to the new president?

The new government came in through the back door. The logical thing would have been for parliament to ratify Mahuad, if it did not want to ratify the coup perpetrated by the military high command and join that coup. We have reservations about how the country can carry on. But as always, we are open to dialogue, but not to a dialogue of fools, in which they talk to us after they have already taken all the decisions. It is necessary to establish a real debate with the whole of society to avoid chicanery. This can only be done through a popular consultation. Let the people decide.

During the uprising of July 1999, the indigenous questioned some Pachakutik members of parliament who were seeking talks with the government without the movement having made a decision about this.

That was right, because members of parliament should listen to their mandate from the indigenous people and they must know they can be removed by them. This was understood by the members of parliament, who have accepted their mistakes and are there to support the [indigenous] movement. They are its representatives in parliament, but they can never replace the direct representation which the organisations themselves had in leading the uprising. So it has to be the organisations themselves who decide if their members of parliament have talks with the government or not.

When you were a member of parliament, you presented various bills which were not given time? What conclusions do you draw from this legislative experience?

Over the course of time we learned that some legislators block bills from outsiders and expect to be offered a sweetener to get them going. The sweetener is not necessarily money, it can be an exchange of favours. I support you today, so you support me tomorrow. We do not agree with this attitude, which is virtually institutionalised in all the powers of the state. We are fighting on from the inside to change this situation, but the solution will not come overnight.

And in any case, we have to say that not all the legislators go along with these institutionalised practices and

therefore, despite everything, it is possible to achieve results.

Can you give examples?

The approval of ILO Agreement 169, on the rights of indigenous peoples, by members of parliament from all sectors, proves that we can often agree on matters which, like this one, are of vital importance for broad sectors of the country. This ratification shows us that all the political sectors represented in parliament agree on pluri-nationality, which is a subject that matters greatly to the indigenous. And it is clear that there are many things on which we can agree.

Another important thing is to demonstrate that parliament can perform a responsible fiscal role, without personal or party interest interfering. We demonstrated that the fight against corruption is possible without it becoming bogged down in party politics. An example is when we denounced the (irregular) use of reserved funds by the ex-government minister César Verduga.

If Pachakutik gets into government will the indigenous movement maintain its independence?

In reality, Pachakutik has much more chance with local government, where it has demonstrated that many things can be done and great gains made for the poor sectors of the population, although we have not given up on being in government. From the moment we stood in the election we have known that there is the possibility of getting into government. But to get there we have to overcome the obstacles in a democracy which only give chances to the rich who can invest in electoral propaganda and manipulate power and the media. These media are difficult for the indigenous movement and the social movements, because they are not at local level in certain regions. As for independence, Pachakutik was created by the social movements and is answerable to them.

Within Pachakutik certain indigenous sectors appear to be interested only in putting forward their own concerns. What do you think about this?

There are two currents in the movement. On the one hand, there is a current deriving from indigenous intellectuals who see everything from an indigenous viewpoint. On the other hand, there is a sector trying to consolidate a joint project with all Ecuadorians, which does not isolate the indigenous movement. This is the sector to which I subscribe.

There is also a third attitude – I would not call it a current. This is the attitude of those who take sides in accordance with their own particular interests, sometimes electoral interests, sometimes for the sake of certain benefits they can obtain if a particular proposal is approved. It is an attitude very tied up with the bureaucratic practices of the old left and which also appeals to certain indigenous. But I believe it has no significance or power within Pachakutik.

At any rate, the first Pachakutik congress, in August 1999, approved a principle that was already assumed by the communities and organisations: the logic of a project that does not exclude anybody, a broad project which was reflected in the recent uprising and popular insurrection.

What is the essence of the current indigenous movement?

We continue to hold our ancestral values, such as the model of community and solidarity, that we have been practicing for hundreds of years. When a family in the community is in a difficult situation, everyone joins together to help it.

Then we have the *minga*, as we call collective work to build a road or a house or to get the harvest in. That is why we say that our movement is in '*minga* for life'.

One of the Ecuadorian indigenous movement's fundamental demands is the declaration of Ecuador as a pluri-national state. This has been interpreted by some sectors as its geographical division into distinct states.

The pluri-national state is one single state with legal plurality in territories occupied by indigenous nations and their right to make political, economic, cultural and social decisions. It does not break up the national territory, but it grants our peoples different levels of decision-making and autonomy, as laid down in Agreement 169.

PART 3

APPENDICES

PAUL SMITH / PANOS PICTURES

Work crew (minga) constructing an adobe wall.

Appendix 1:

INDIGENOUS PLURINATIONAL MANDATE

This mandate addresses the principal needs of the indigenous people of Ecuador, which we present to the Ecuadorian state, as an urgent proposal to be implemented through compensatory measures in the face of the recent economic measures.

1. JURIDICAL POLICY

1.1 Constitutional recognition of the Plurinational and Pluricultural character of the Ecuadorian State.

1.2 Ratification of Agreement 169 of the ILO, concerning Indigenous and Tribal Peoples.

1.3 Reform of the Municipal Regulations Law, referring to the Non-Payment of Rural Property Taxes.

1.4 A share of 1 per cent of the cost-per-barrel of oil exploited in the territories of the indigenous peoples.

1.5 Amnesty for prisoners and penal defendants who have been sentenced as a result of the fight for land or in defense of land.

1.6 Revision of the signed agreements between Religious Missions and the Government that refer to indigenous peoples.

1.7 The Government, the National Congress and the Supreme Court of Justice, must express their disagreement with the commemorations of the quincentennary, and ask an indemnity for damages of the Spanish government and the European Economic Community, which should be used for the benefit of the indigenous people and popular sector.

2. ECONOMY AND PRODUCTION

2.1 Creation of a fund in the amount of 10 billion *sucres* annually to settle land disputes.

2.2 Delimitation and legalisation of the ancestral territories of the indigenous peoples within parks and natural reserves throughout the country.

2.3 Creation of a Special Indigenous Fund for Integrated Development Programmes.

2.4 Freezing of the prices of necessary industrial products as well as of machinery and fertilisers.

3. EDUCATION AND CULTURE

3.1 Continuation of the Bilingual and Intercultural Education Programme, properly financed and with respect to the administrative, technical and financial autonomy of the National Directorate of Bilingual and Intercultural Education.

3.2 Respect for and continuation of the Agreement signed by CONAIE and the Ministry of Education, as well as for other cultural programmes, infrastructural projects, etc.

3.3 Establishment of scholarships to support the training of indigenous students.

3.4 We call for the Bilingual and Intercultural Education Programme to be directed towards all of Ecuadorian society. The government proposal should not be limited to the learning of the Quechua language alone, but should include the study of the different peoples that constitute Ecuador.

C O N A I E
Friday 13 November 1992

Appendix 2

C169 INDIGENOUS AND TRIBAL PEOPLES CONVENTION, 1989

Convention concerning Indigenous and Tribal Peoples in Independent Countries

(Date of coming into force: 05:09:1991.)
Convention: C169

Copyright © 1999 International Labour Organization (ILO)
webinfo@ilo.org
Source: ILO database ILOLEX
http://ilolex.ilo.ch:1567/public/english/docs/convdisp.htm

Article 1

1. This Convention applies to:

(a) tribal peoples in independent countries whose social, cultural and economic conditions distinguish them from other sections of the national community, and whose status is regulated wholly or partially by their own customs or traditions or by special laws or regulations;

(b) peoples in independent countries who are regarded as indigenous on account of their descent from the populations which inhabited the country, or a geographical region to which the country belongs, at the time of conquest or colonisation or the establishment of present state boundaries and who, irrespective of their legal status, retain some or all of their own social, economic, cultural and political institutions.

2. Self-identification as indigenous or tribal shall be regarded as a fundamental criterion for determining the groups to which the provisions of this Convention apply.

[...]

Article 2

1. Governments shall have the responsibility for developing, with the participation of the peoples concerned, co-ordinated and systematic action to protect the rights of these peoples and to guarantee respect for their integrity.

2. Such action shall include measures for:

(a) ensuring that members of these peoples benefit on an equal footing from the rights and opportunities which national laws and regulations grant to other members of the population;

(b) promoting the full realisation of the social, economic and cultural rights of these peoples with respect for their social and cultural identity, their customs and traditions and their institutions;

(c) assisting the members of the peoples concerned to eliminate socio-economic gaps that may exist between indigenous and other members of the national community, in a manner compatible with their aspirations and ways of life.

Article 3

1. Indigenous and tribal peoples shall enjoy the full measure of human rights and fundamental freedoms without hindrance or discrimination. The provisions of the Convention shall be applied without discrimination to male and female members of these peoples.

2. No form of force or coercion shall be used in violation of the human rights and fundamental freedoms of the peoples concerned, including the rights contained in this Convention.

Article 4

1. Special measures shall be adopted as appropriate for safeguarding the persons, institutions, property, labour, cultures and environment of the peoples concerned.

2. Such special measures shall not be contrary to the freely-expressed wishes of the peoples concerned.

3. Enjoyment of the general rights of citizenship, without discrimination, shall not be prejudiced in any way by such special measures.

Article 5

In applying the provisions of this Convention:

(a) the social, cultural, religious and spiritual values and practices of these peoples shall be recognised and protected, and due account shall be taken of the nature of the problems which face them both as groups and as individuals;

(b) the integrity of the values, practices and institutions of these peoples shall be respected;

(c) policies aimed at mitigating the difficulties experienced by these peoples in facing new conditions of life and work shall be adopted, with the participation and co-operation of the peoples affected.

Article 6

1. In applying the provisions of this Convention, governments shall:

(a) consult the peoples concerned, through appropriate procedures and in particular through their representative institutions, whenever consideration is being given to legislative or administrative measures which may affect them directly;

(b) establish means by which these peoples can freely participate, to at least the same extent as other sectors of the population, at all levels of decision-making in elective institutions and administrative and other bodies responsible for policies and programmes which concern them;

(c) establish means for the full development of these peoples' own institutions and initiatives, and in appropriate cases provide the resources necessary for this purpose.

2. The consultations carried out in application of this Convention shall be undertaken, in good faith and in a form appropriate to the circumstances, with the objective of achieving agreement or consent to the proposed measures.

Article 7

1. The peoples concerned shall have the right to decide their own priorities for the process of development as it affects their lives, beliefs, institutions and spiritual well-being and the lands they occupy or otherwise use, and to exercise control, to the extent possible, over their own economic, social and cultural development. In addition, they shall participate in the formulation, implementation and evaluation of plans and programmes for national and regional development which may affect them directly.

2. The improvement of the conditions of life and work and levels of health and education of the peoples concerned, with their participation and co-operation, shall be a matter of priority in plans for the overall economic development of areas they inhabit. Special projects for development of the areas in question shall also be so designed as to promote such improvement.

3. Governments shall ensure that, whenever appropriate, studies are carried out, in co-operation with the peoples concerned, to assess the social, spiritual, cultural and environmental impact on them of planned development activities. The results of these studies shall be considered as fundamental criteria for the implementation of these activities.

4. Governments shall take measures, in co-operation with the peoples concerned, to protect and preserve the environment of the territories they inhabit.

Article 8

1. In applying national laws and regulations to the peoples concerned, due regard shall be had to their customs or customary laws.

2. These peoples shall have the right to retain their own customs and institutions, where these are not incompatible with fundamental rights defined by the national legal system and with internationally recognised human rights. Procedures shall be established, whenever necessary, to resolve conflicts which may arise in the application of this principle.

3. The application of paragraphs 1 and 2 of this Article shall not prevent members of these peoples from exercising the rights granted to all citizens and from assuming the corresponding duties.

Article 9

1. To the extent compatible with the national legal system and internationally recognised human rights, the methods customarily practised by the peoples concerned for dealing with offences committed by their members shall be respected.

2. The customs of these peoples in regard to penal matters shall be taken into consideration by the authorities and courts dealing with such cases.

Article 10

1. In imposing penalties laid down by general law on members of these peoples account shall be taken of their economic, social and cultural characteristics.

2. Preference shall be given to methods of punishment other than confinement in prison.

Article 11

The exaction from members of the peoples concerned of compulsory personal services in any form, whether paid or unpaid, shall be prohibited and punishable by law, except in cases prescribed by law for all citizens.

Article 12

The peoples concerned shall be safeguarded against the abuse of their rights and shall be able to take legal proceedings, either individually or through their representative bodies, for the effective protection of these rights. Measures shall be taken to ensure that members of these peoples can understand and be understood in legal proceedings, where necessary through the provision of interpretation or by other effective means.

Part II. Land

Article 13

1. In applying the provisions of this Part of the Convention governments shall respect the special importance for the cultures and spiritual values of the peoples concerned of their relationship with the lands or territories, or both as applicable, which they occupy or otherwise use, and in particular the collective aspects of this relationship.

2. The use of the term lands in Articles 15 and 16 shall include the concept of territories, which covers the total environment of the areas which the peoples concerned occupy or otherwise use.

Article 14

1. The rights of ownership and possession of the peoples concerned over the lands which they traditionally occupy shall be recognised. In addition, measures shall be taken in appropriate cases to safeguard the right of the peoples concerned to use lands not exclusively occupied by them, but to which they have traditionally had access for their subsistence and traditional activities. Particular attention shall be paid to the situation of nomadic peoples and shifting cultivators in this respect.

2. Governments shall take steps as necessary to identify the lands which the peoples concerned traditionally occupy, and to guarantee effective protection of their rights of ownership and possession.

3. Adequate procedures shall be established within the national legal system to resolve land claims by the peoples concerned.

Article 15

1. The rights of the peoples concerned to the natural resources pertaining to their lands shall be specially safeguarded. These rights include the right of these peoples to participate in the use, management and conservation of these resources.

2. In cases in which the State retains the ownership of mineral or sub-surface resources or rights to other resources pertaining to lands, governments shall establish or maintain procedures through which they shall consult these peoples, with a view to ascertaining whether and to what degree their interests would be prejudiced, before undertaking or
permitting any programmes for the exploration or exploitation of such

resources pertaining to their lands. The peoples concerned shall wherever possible participate in the benefits of such activities, and shall receive fair compensation for any damages which they may sustain as a result of such activities.

Article 16

1. Subject to the following paragraphs of this Article, the peoples concerned shall not be removed from the lands which they occupy.

2. Where the relocation of these peoples is considered necessary as an exceptional measure, such relocation shall take place only with their free and informed consent. Where their consent cannot be obtained, such relocation shall take place only following appropriate procedures established by national laws and regulations, including public inquiries where appropriate, which provide the opportunity for effective representation of the peoples concerned.

3. Whenever possible, these peoples shall have the right to return to their traditional lands, as soon as the grounds for relocation cease to exist.

4. When such return is not possible, as determined by agreement or, in the absence of such agreement, through appropriate procedures, these peoples shall be provided in all possible cases with lands of quality and legal status at least equal to that of the lands previously occupied by them, suitable to provide for their present needs and future development. Where the peoples concerned express a preference for compensation in money or in kind, they shall be so compensated under appropriate guarantees.

5. Persons thus relocated shall be fully compensated for any resulting loss or injury.

Article 17

1. Procedures established by the peoples concerned for the transmission of land rights among members of these peoples shall be respected.

2. The peoples concerned shall be consulted whenever consideration is being given to their capacity to alienate their lands or otherwise transmit their rights outside their own community.

3. Persons not belonging to these peoples shall be prevented from taking advantage of their customs or of lack of understanding of the laws on the part of their members to secure the ownership, possession or use of land belonging to them.

Article 18

Adequate penalties shall be established by law for unauthorised intrusion upon, or use of, the lands of the peoples concerned, and governments shall take measures to prevent such offences.

Article 19

National agrarian programmes shall secure to the peoples concerned treatment equivalent to that accorded to other sectors of the population with regard to: (a) the provision of more land for these peoples when they have not the area necessary for providing the essentials of a normal existence, or for any possible increase in their numbers; (b) the provision of the means required to promote the development of the lands which these peoples already possess.

[...]

Part IV. Vocational Training, Handicrafts and Rural Industries

Article 21

Members of the peoples concerned shall enjoy opportunities at least equal to those of other citizens in respect of vocational training measures.

Article 22

1. Measures shall be taken to promote the voluntary participation of members of the peoples concerned in vocational training programmes of general application.

2. Whenever existing programmes of vocational training of general application do not meet the special needs of the peoples concerned, governments shall, with the participation of these peoples, ensure the provision of special training programmes and facilities.

3. Any special training programmes shall be based on the economic environment, social and cultural conditions and practical needs of the peoples concerned. Any studies made in this connection shall be carried out in co-operation with these peoples, who shall be consulted on the organisation and operation of such programmes. Where feasible, these peoples shall progressively assume responsibility for the organisation and operation of such special training programmes, if they so decide.

Article 23

1. Handicrafts, rural and community-based industries, and subsistence economy and traditional activities of the peoples concerned, such as hunting, fishing, trapping and gathering, shall be recognised as important factors in the maintenance of their cultures and in their economic self-reliance and development. Governments shall, with the participation of these people and whenever appropriate, ensure that these activities are strengthened and promoted.

2. Upon the request of the peoples concerned, appropriate technical and financial assistance shall be provided wherever possible, taking into account the traditional technologies and cultural characteristics of these peoples, as well as the importance of sustainable and equitable development.

Part V. Social Security and Health

Article 24

Social security schemes shall be extended progressively to cover the peoples concerned, and applied without discrimination against them.

Article 25

1. Governments shall ensure that adequate health services are made available to the peoples concerned, or shall provide them with resources to allow them to design and deliver such services under their own responsibility and control, so that they may enjoy the highest attainable standard of physical and mental health.

2. Health services shall, to the extent possible, be community-based. These services shall be planned and administered in co-operation with the peoples concerned and take into account their economic, geographic, social and cultural conditions as well as their traditional preventive care, healing practices and medicines.

3. The health care system shall give preference to the training and employment of local community health workers, and focus on primary health care while maintaining strong links with other levels of health care services.

4. The provision of such health services shall be co-ordinated with other social, economic and cultural measures in the country.

Part VI. Education and Means of Communication

Article 26

Measures shall be taken to ensure that members of the peoples concerned have the opportunity to acquire education at all levels on at least an equal footing with the rest of the national community.

Article 27

1. Education programmes and services for the peoples concerned shall be developed and implemented in co-operation with them to address their special needs, and shall incorporate their histories, their knowledge and technologies, their value systems and their further social, economic and cultural aspirations.

2. The competent authority shall ensure the training of members of these peoples and their involvement in the formulation and implementation of education programmes, with a view to the progressive transfer of responsibility for the conduct of these programmes to these peoples as appropriate.

3. In addition, governments shall recognise the right of these peoples to establish their own educational institutions and facilities, provided that such institutions meet minimum standards established by the competent authority in consultation with these peoples. Appropriate resources shall be provided for this purpose.

Article 28

1. Children belonging to the peoples concerned shall, wherever practicable, be taught to read and write in their own indigenous language or in the language most commonly used by the group to which they belong. When this is not practicable, the competent authorities shall undertake consultations with these peoples with a view to the adoption of measures to achieve this objective.

2. Adequate measures shall be taken to ensure that these peoples have the opportunity to attain fluency in the national language or in one of the official languages of the country.

3. Measures shall be taken to preserve and promote the development and practice of the indigenous languages of the peoples concerned.

Article 29

The imparting of general knowledge and skills that will help children belonging to the peoples concerned to participate fully and on an equal footing in their own community and in the national community shall be an aim of education for these peoples.

Article 30

1. Governments shall adopt measures appropriate to the traditions and cultures of the peoples concerned, to make known to them their rights and duties, especially in regard to labour, economic opportunities, education and health matters, social welfare and their rights deriving from this Convention.

2. If necessary, this shall be done by means of written translations and through the use of mass communications in the languages of these peoples.

Article 31

Educational measures shall be taken among all sections of the national community, and particularly among those that are in most direct contact with the peoples concerned, with the object of eliminating prejudices that they may harbour in respect of these peoples. To this end, efforts shall be made to ensure that history textbooks and other educational materials provide a fair, accurate and informative portrayal of the societies and cultures of these peoples.

[...]

Part VIII. Administration
Article 33

1. The governmental authority responsible for the matters covered in this Convention shall ensure that agencies or other appropriate mechanisms exist to administer the programmes affecting the peoples concerned, and shall ensure that they have the means necessary for the proper fulfilment of the functions assigned to them.

2. These programmes shall include:
(a) the planning, co-ordination, execution and evaluation, in co-operation with the peoples concerned, of the measures provided for in this Convention;
(b) the proposing of legislative and other measures to the competent authorities and supervision of the application of the measures taken, in co-operation with the peoples concerned.

Appendix 3

BIBLIOGRAPHY/ FURTHER READING

Acosta Alberto et al, *Dolarización*, Abya Yala-ILDIS, Quito, 1996.

Acosta Alberto et al, *Un continente contra la deuda*, Abya Yala-ILDIS, Quito, 1999.

Alta Virginia, López-Bassols MA, Iturralde Nieto Isabel Ma, and various authors, *Estado en América* Latina, Abya Yala, Quito, 1998.

Almeida Ileana et al, *En defensa del pluralismo y la igualdad*, Abya Yala, Quito, 1999.

Americas Watch, *La violencia continúa*, Tercer Mundo, Bogotá, 1993.

Báez Sara et al, *Cotacachi*, Abya Yala, Quito, 1999.

Bravo Elizabeth, *Biodiversidad y derechos de los pueblos*, Abya Yala, Quito, 1996.

Camú Urzúa G y Tótoro Taulis D, *EZLN: El ejército que salió de la selva*, Planeta, Mexico, 1994.

Carvalho-Neto Paulo, *Arte popular del Ecuador*, Abya Yala, Quito, 1989.

Centro de Cultura de Wasak'entza, *Chamanismo y simbolismo onírico en el pueblo achuar*, Abya Yala, Quito, 1998.

Checa Fernando, *Jumandi*, Programa número 22, Proyecto Corades-Todas las voces, CIESPAL, Quito 1989.

Chumpi kayap Maria Magdalena, *Los ament: expresión religiosa y familiar de los shuar*, Abya Yala, Quito, 1985.

CONAIE, *Las nacionalidades indigenas y sus derechos colectivos en la constiutución*, Quito, 1999.

De la Torre Luis, *Experiencia de educación intercultural bilingue en Latinoamérica*, Abya Yala, Quito, 1998.

Galeano Eduardo, *Memoria del fuego I: Los nacimientos*, Ediciones del chanchito, Montevideo 1987.

Galich Manuel, *Nuestros primeros padres*, Casa de las Américas, Havana 1979.

Galindo Alberto Flores, *El nudo colonial*, Revista Cultura Popular número 10, Lima 1985.

Garces Enrique, *Daquilema, Rex: Biografía de un dolor índio*, Edición Casa de la Cultura Ecuatoriana, Quito 1961.

Economist Intelligence Unit, *Ecuador Country Profile 1999-2000*, London 1999.

Ediciones del Nuevo Mundo, *Popol Vuh: Mitos y leyendas del pueblo Quiché*, Montevideo 1987.

Editorial Lumen, *Guía del Mundo*, Buenos Aires 1998.

Fericgla Josep M, *Al trasluz de la ayahuasca*, Abya Yala, Quito, 1997.

Fondo de Cultura Económica, *Libro de los libros del Chilam-Balam*, Mexico 1948.

Frank Edwin, Patiño Ninfa, Rodríguez Martha, *Los políticos y los indígenas*, Abya Yala, Quito, 1992.

Friedrich Hassaurek, *Cuatro años entre los ecuatorianos*, Abya Yala, Quito, 1993

García Canclini Nestor, *Culturas híbridas*, Grijalbo, Mexico, 1999.

Instituto del Tercer Mundo, *The World Guide*, New Internationalist Publications, Oxford, 1997.

Instituto Otavaleño de Antropología, *Los Quijos*, Otavalo 1980.

International Labour Organisation, Convention 169 of the International Labour Organisation (ILO).

Juncosa José, *Agenda UNOPAC 1990*, Editorial Abya-Yala, Quito 1990.

Kleymeyer Carlos David, *Imashi, Imashi: Adivinanzas poéticas de los campesinos indígenas del mundo andino*, Abya Yala, Quito, 1996.

Larrea Fernando *Organizaciones campesinas e indígenas y poderes locales*, Abya Yala, Quito, 1999.

Larrea Fernando *Propuesta para la gestión participativa del desarrollo local*, RIAD, Quito, 1999.

Lewin Boleslao, *La insurrección de Tupac Amaru*, EUDEBA, Buenos Aires 1963.

Lluco Miguel et al, *Una minga por la vida (Crédito para los pobres del campo)*, Abya Yala, Quito, 1998.

Lucas Kintto *Rebeliones indígenas y negras en América Latina*, Abya Yala, Quito, 1992.

Lucas Kintto *Mujeres del Siglo XX*, Abya Yala, Quito, 1997.

Macas Luis et al, *Los derechos de los pueblos indios y el Estado (58)*, Abya Yala, Quito, 1998.

Mires Fernando, *El discurso de la indianidad*, Abya Yala, Quito, 1992.

Moncada José et al, *Crisis privatización y sindicalismo*, Fundación José Peralta, Quito, 1992.

Moncayo Paco et al, *Fuerzas Armadas Desarrollo y Democrácia*, Abya Yala, Quito, 1996.

Morales Rodas Raquel, *Dolores Cacuango*, Proyecto EBIGtz, Quito, 1998.

Moreno Yanez Segundo, *Sublevaciones indígenas en la audiencia de Quito*, University of Bonn, Bonn, 1976.

Muller-Plantenberg Clarita, *Derechos, económicos, sociales y culturales de los pueblos indígenas*, GhK ELNI-Abya Yala, Quito, 1999.

Oliva de Coll J, *La resistencia indígena ante la conquista*, Siglo XXI, Mexico, 1974.

Ortíz T Pablo, *Globalización y conflictos socioambientales*, Abya Yala, Quito, 1997.

Pellizaro Rolf, Arutam: *Mitología shuar*, Abya Yala, Quito, 1996.

Pizarro León Gómez, *Las FARC 1949-1966*, Tercer Mundo, Bogotá, 1992.

Rodríguez Antonio et al, *Encuentro sobre poderes locales alternativos*, ECUARUNARI, Quito, 1998.

Rodríguez J Lourdes, Barrera G Augusto, Gallegos R Franklin, *Ecuador: un modelo para (des)armar*, Centro de Investigaciones Ciudad, Quito, 1999.

Roos Wilma, Omer van Renterghem, *Ecuador: A guide to the people, politics and culture*, Latin America Bureau, London 1997.

Sabanes Pou Dafne et al, *Actores de Cambio en América Latina*, Noticias Aliadas, Lima, 1999.

Ulcuango Ricardo et al, *Historia de ECUARUNARI*, ECUARUNARI, Quito, 1998.

Vallejo Raúl, *Crónica mestiza del nuevo Poachakuyik*, University of Maryland, 1996.

Varea Ana María et al, *Biodiversidad, Bioprospección y Bioseguridad*, Abya Yala, Quito, 1997.

Varea Ana María et al, *Desarrollo Ecoilógico* (Tres Tomos), Abya Yala, Quito, 1997

Villamil José et al, *Identidad nacional y globalización*, ILDIS, Quito, 1997.

Whymper Edward, *Viaje a través de los majestuosos Andes del Ecuador*, Abya Yala, Quito, 1993.

WOLA (Washington Office for Latin America), *Peligro inminente: Las fuerzas armadas de Estados Unidos y la guerra contra las drogas*, Tercer Mundo, Bogotá, 1992.

Zibechi Raúl, *Los arroyos cuando bajan (Los desafíos del zapatismo)*, Nordam, Montevideo, 1995.

DAILY PAPERS

El Comercio, Hoy, Expreso, El Universo (Ecuador); *El Colombiano, El Espectador, El Tiempo* (Colombia); *La República* (Peru); *The Washington Post, The New York Times, The Wall Street Journal, The Miami Herald* (United States).

REVIEWS

Pachakutik, ALAI, Gestión (Ecuador); *Sem Terra* (Brasil); *Brecha* (Uruguay); *Ko'eyu Latinoamericano* (Venezuela).

PERIODICALS

Richarikzun, Qué Fue, Derechos del Pueblo (Ecuador); *Notcias Aliadas* (Peru).

NEWS AGENCIES

Inter Press Service (IPS); Servicio Informativo de la Organización de Estados Iberoamericanos para la Educación la Ciencia y la Cultura (OEI).

BULLETINS

Instituto Científico de Culturas Indígenas (ICCI), CONAIE, ECUARUNARI.

WEBSITES

Oilwach, Acción Ecológica, Comisión Ecuménica de Derechos Humanos, Confederación de Afiliados al Seguro Campesino, CONAIE.

Appendix 4
ORGANISATIONS

Organización Ambientalista Accion Ecológica:
amazonia@hoy.net; verde@hoy.net;
www.ecuanex.net.ec/accion/

Confederación de Nacionalidades Indígenas del Ecuador (CONAIE):
conaie@ecuanex.net.ec;
conaie.nativeweb.org/

Confederación de Pueblos de la Nacionalidad Kichwa (ECUARUNARI):
riccharishun@yahoo.com;
kichua@ecuanex.net.ec

Confederación Unica de Afiliados al Seguro Social Campesino – Coordinadora Nacional Campesina (CONFEUNASSC-CNC):
ssc-cnc@campesinos-fmlgt.org.ec

Movimiento de Unidad Plurinacional Pachakutik-Nuevo País (MUPP-NP):
pachakutik@waccom.net.ec

Asamblea Permanente por los Derechos Humanos (APDH):
quijote@gyeunix1.porta.net

Comisión Ecuménica de Derechos Humanos (CEDHU).
cedhu@ecuanex.net.ec;
www.derechos.net/cedhu/

Instituto Científico de Culturas Indígenas:
icci@waccom.net.ec
www.icci.nativeweb.org

Centro Cultural Abya Yala:
editorial@abyayala.org;
www.abyayala.org

Instituto Latinoamericano de Investigaciones Sociales:
ildis1@ECNET.ec